I0005943

The Future of Work

How Automation and Robotics Are Changing Industries What jobs will look like in a world dominated by robots

THOMPSON CARTER

All rights reserved

No part of this book may be reproduced, distributed, or transmitted in any form or by any means without the prior written permission of the publisher, except in the case of brief quotations embodied in critical reviews and certain other noncommercial uses permitted by right law.

Table of Content

TABLE OF CONTENTS

Introduction

Navigating the Future of Work in an Automated World

The world is on the cusp of an extraordinary transformation. Advances in **automation**, **robotics**, and **artificial intelligence (AI)** are rapidly reshaping industries, economies, and the very nature of work. From **self-driving cars** and **autonomous robots** in warehouses to **AI-driven software** managing complex data sets, the workplace is becoming increasingly dominated by machines that are capable of performing tasks traditionally reserved for humans. What does this mean for the future of work? How will automation affect the millions of workers whose jobs are at risk of being replaced? Will it enhance human capabilities, or will it lead to mass unemployment? The answers to these questions are shaping the future of our economy, society, and individual lives.

In this book, we will explore the vast implications of automation and robotics in the workplace, diving into the **technological innovations** that are revolutionizing industries and the **psychological, economic, and social**

consequences that come with these changes. From manufacturing and logistics to healthcare and creative industries, we will examine how automation is already reshaping the way work is done and speculate on the next steps for this evolving trend.

As automation continues to penetrate deeper into the workforce, it is important to recognize that these technologies are not simply replacing human labor—they are **augmenting human capabilities** and opening up new possibilities for productivity, creativity, and efficiency. At the same time, these advancements also present complex challenges. The transition to an automated future raises concerns about **job displacement**, **income inequality**, **worker well-being**, and **social justice**. How do we ensure that the benefits of automation are shared equitably across society? How can we support workers whose roles are made obsolete by robots? And what ethical considerations must be addressed as AI and automation become more autonomous?

This book aims to answer these questions by providing a comprehensive look at the state of automation in the workforce, its potential to reshape industries, and the new realities workers will face in an increasingly robotic world. The chapters are designed to be both informative and forward-looking, offering **real-world examples, success stories**, and **insights** into the challenges and opportunities automation brings. From large corporations like **Amazon** and **Tesla** to small businesses embracing **robotic process automation (RPA)**, we'll explore how different sectors are integrating automation and the positive outcomes they have achieved.

We will also examine the psychological impact of automation on workers, exploring how it influences **job satisfaction, mental health**, and **worker engagement**. As automation takes over repetitive tasks, human workers will be freed to focus on more complex, creative, and strategic roles, but how will this shift affect their sense of **purpose** and **identity**? How can employers and governments support the mental well-being of employees navigating an ever-changing job landscape?

In the chapters ahead, we will take a closer look at **the role of government** in regulating automation, protecting workers, and ensuring a **smooth transition** into an automated future. Additionally, we will discuss the **ethical challenges** posed by automation—how we balance the efficiency gains of machines with the protection of human labor and dignity.

The goal of this book is not to offer a dystopian view of the future, nor to blindly embrace a future dominated by machines. Instead, we aim to offer a nuanced perspective that acknowledges the potential benefits and challenges of automation while emphasizing the importance of thoughtful integration and **ethical considerations** in this new world of work. Automation is a tool—a powerful one—but it is ultimately human decisions, governance, and values that will determine how it impacts society. We are entering a pivotal moment in history, and the choices we make today will shape the future of work for generations to come.

As we move forward into this era of technological advancement, it is crucial that we prepare for the future of work with **flexibility, resilience**, and a shared commitment to making sure automation serves the needs of all people. This book will explore how we can build a future where **humans and robots work together**, and where technology enables workers to thrive, not just survive.

Let us embark on this journey to understand the role of **automation** in shaping our working world and the possibilities it opens for a more innovative, efficient, and inclusive future.

CHAPTER 1

INTRODUCTION TO AUTOMATION AND ROBOTICS

Overview of Automation and Robotics

In this chapter, we will start by defining what automation and robotics are and why they are so important in today's world. Automation refers to the use of technology to perform tasks without human intervention, while robotics involves designing and using robots—machines that can perform tasks automatically, often with a high degree of precision. The integration of these technologies is reshaping industries across the globe, and understanding their evolution is key to grasping the future of work.

What Is Automation?

Automation can be as simple as using a machine to perform a repetitive task that was once done by humans, like a conveyor belt in a factory. Today, automation is much more complex. It involves the use of artificial intelligence (AI), machine learning, and advanced software to perform tasks that require decision-making and problem-solving.

What Is Robotics?

Robotics is a subfield of automation, but with a focus on creating machines (robots) that can interact with the environment in a way that mimics human action. Robots are designed to automate tasks that might be too dangerous, repetitive, or precise for humans. For example, robots are commonly used in manufacturing lines, healthcare surgeries, and even at home as robotic vacuum cleaners.

The Evolution of Automation and Robotics

Automation has been around for centuries. The first recorded use of automated machines dates back to ancient Greece, with devices powered by water and steam. However, it wasn't until the 20th century that automation took off, particularly with the advent of the assembly line, popularized by Henry Ford in the early 1900s. This allowed for mass production, lowering costs, and increasing productivity.

As we moved into the 21st century, the evolution of computing and digital technology enabled robots and automated systems to perform increasingly complex tasks. Manufacturing robots, for example, can now assemble products with incredible precision, while advanced AI systems in software can predict customer behaviors or optimize traffic patterns in smart cities.

The Impact on Industries

Automation and robotics have had a profound impact on many industries. In manufacturing, robots now assemble cars, make electronics, and produce medical equipment. In agriculture, autonomous machines harvest crops and monitor fields, reducing the need for manual labor. In logistics, automated systems transport goods through warehouses and deliver packages directly to customers.

However, these advancements come with both positive and negative effects. On the positive side, automation increases efficiency, reduces costs, and improves safety. Robots can work tirelessly in dangerous or unhealthy environments, performing tasks like welding, lifting heavy objects, or handling hazardous materials.

On the other hand, automation can lead to job displacement. As machines take over routine tasks, there is a growing concern about the future of human workers. Industries are being forced to rethink the nature of work, and employees may need to acquire new skills to remain competitive.

Why Does This Matter?

The impact of automation and robotics on industries is far-reaching. It is changing the way businesses operate, how products are made, and even how consumers interact with services. As robots become more advanced, they are also taking on tasks that were once thought to be reserved for humans, such as customer service or decision-making roles in finance.

This chapter sets the stage for understanding how these technologies are transforming industries and jobs. In the coming chapters, we will explore specific sectors that are being revolutionized by automation and robotics and discuss the future of work in a world where robots play a larger role.

By understanding the basics of automation and robotics, their history, and their impact, readers will be better equipped to navigate the changes that are already underway in the workplace.

This introduction gives readers an accessible overview of the technologies and sets the tone for the rest of the book. Let me know if you'd like any adjustments or further details!

CHAPTER 2

THE EVOLUTION OF WORK AND TECHNOLOGY

How Work Has Evolved Over the Years

Work has transformed dramatically over the past few centuries, from agrarian societies where most people worked on farms to industrialized cities filled with factories and offices. This chapter takes a look at the key phases in the evolution of work and how technological advancements have played a pivotal role in shaping job markets.

The Pre-Industrial Era: Agricultural and Craft-Based Work

Before the Industrial Revolution, most people lived in rural areas and worked in agriculture. Farms were the primary place of work, and people relied on manual labor for tasks such as planting, harvesting, and livestock management. During this time, jobs were often specialized, passed down through generations, and performed in small-scale, community-based settings.

15

In addition to farming, there was also a growing number of skilled craftworkers—blacksmiths, weavers, potters, and carpenters—who created goods by hand. Work was deeply connected to local communities, with long hours of labor often dictated by the seasons or the needs of the family.

The Industrial Revolution: The Rise of Mass Production and Factories

The Industrial Revolution, which began in the late 18th century, radically changed the nature of work. The introduction of machinery in factories allowed for mass production, which could be done faster and more efficiently than by hand. Steam power, mechanized looms, and factory assembly lines transformed industries like textiles, coal, iron, and steel, dramatically increasing production levels.

This period marked the shift from agrarian and craft-based work to factory work. Workers moved to urban areas in search of jobs, which led to the growth of cities and the establishment of industrial economies. Factory jobs were often monotonous and required workers to operate machinery, making the work more specialized and less personal than in the past.

The Early 20th Century: Automation Begins to Take Hold

The early 20th century saw the introduction of more sophisticated automation. Henry Ford's assembly line revolutionized the automobile industry by drastically increasing production efficiency. Ford's system relied on standardized, repetitive tasks that allowed workers to perform their job faster and with less skill required. This shift created a new era of mass production and increased the demand for factory workers.

Technology also began to penetrate other industries. For example, in agriculture, tractors and other mechanized tools replaced manual labor, allowing farmers to produce more crops with fewer workers. However, as technology advanced, jobs that were once done manually became more automated, leading to the need for new skill sets.

Post-World War II: The Rise of Office and Service Jobs

After World War II, there was a shift away from industrial work toward service-oriented and office-based jobs. Technology such as computers, telephones, and fax machines made it possible for people to work from offices and perform tasks that required more cognitive and technical skills.

The post-war economic boom created a demand for workers in sectors like finance, healthcare, and education. While factories continued to employ large numbers of people, the expansion of white-collar jobs led to the growth of industries focused on communication, information processing, and customer service. This was the beginning of the "knowledge economy" where intellectual capital became just as important as physical labor.

The Late 20th Century: The Digital Revolution

The latter half of the 20th century saw the rise of computers, the internet, and software, which began to redefine how work was conducted. The digital revolution changed almost every industry, from finance (with online banking and trading) to retail (with e-commerce and online shopping). The introduction of personal computers, and later, smartphones and tablets, allowed workers to access information and perform tasks remotely.

The late 20th century also saw the rise of automation in office work. Software programs replaced paper-based tasks, and more advanced automation systems began to take on administrative roles. This reduced the need for human intervention in many clerical jobs, but also created new positions in IT, data analysis, and digital marketing.

The 21st Century: The Age of Artificial Intelligence and Robotics

In the 21st century, we have entered the era of artificial intelligence (AI), robotics, and advanced automation technologies. These innovations are now taking over jobs that were once thought to require human intelligence, such as driving, diagnosing diseases, or even making creative decisions.

AI and machine learning systems can now analyze vast amounts of data and perform tasks that require decision-making, pattern recognition, and problem-solving. This is leading to job displacement in industries like transportation (e.g., autonomous vehicles), retail (e.g., cashierless stores), and even healthcare (e.g., robotic surgery). Meanwhile, robots are taking over physically demanding or dangerous tasks in fields like manufacturing, mining, and logistics.

How Technological Advancements Have Shaped Job Markets

As technology evolves, the job market continues to shift. The rise of automation, AI, and robotics has caused job displacement in some sectors, but it has also created new opportunities in emerging fields like data science, robotics engineering, AI programming, and cyber security. Many jobs now require a higher level of education and technical skill, which has led to a growing demand for STEM (science, technology, engineering, and mathematics) workers.

Moreover, the gig economy has emerged alongside advancements in technology, with platforms like Uber, Airbnb, and TaskRabbit offering flexible, short-term work opportunities. Technology has enabled a new type of worker—someone who can create their own schedule and work remotely, often without traditional job benefits like health insurance or retirement plans.

However, while technology has created new opportunities, it has also raised challenges for workers who are displaced by automation. The shift from manual labor to knowledge-based work requires workers to constantly adapt and learn new skills. As the pace of technological change accelerates, continuous learning and reskilling have become essential for staying relevant in the job market.

Conclusion: What's Next for Work?

The evolution of work is far from over. As automation and robotics continue to develop, the nature of jobs and the skills required to perform them will keep changing. In the next chapter, we will explore how automation is already transforming industries like manufacturing, healthcare, and retail—and how workers in these fields are adapting to the new landscape.

This chapter lays the foundation for understanding how work has evolved and prepares readers for the deep dive into the specific effects of automation and robotics on different sectors in later chapters. Let me know if you'd like any modifications!

CHAPTER 3

THE RISE OF AUTOMATION IN THE WORKPLACE

Introduction to Automation in the Workplace

In this chapter, we will explore how automation is making its way into workplaces across various industries, transforming the way tasks are performed and reshaping the workforce. From the manufacturing floor to customer service centers, automation is increasingly being integrated into everyday business operations. Understanding how automation is adopted in different industries helps us gain insight into its potential benefits, challenges, and future impact.

Automation in Manufacturing: Efficiency and Precision

Manufacturing has been one of the first and most significant sectors to embrace automation. The introduction of automated systems in factories has dramatically changed how products are made, increasing speed, reducing human error, and lowering production costs. Automation in manufacturing started with mechanical systems like conveyor belts and assembly lines. Over time, robots and computer-controlled machines have taken over tasks like welding, painting, and packaging.

Today, automated systems are capable of performing highly complex tasks. For instance, robots can assemble intricate electronics, while automated machines are used to sort, inspect, and even pack products with great precision. This shift has allowed manufacturers to scale production rapidly and maintain consistent quality across large volumes of products.

Automated Quality Control

One key area in manufacturing where automation has excelled is quality control. Automated inspection systems, powered by advanced cameras and sensors, can detect flaws or defects in products at a much higher speed and accuracy than humans. For example, in the automotive industry, robots are used to scan car parts for any imperfections, ensuring that only products that meet the required standards make it to the assembly line. This kind of automation reduces waste and improves product reliability.

Automation in the Service Sector: Enhancing Customer Experience

While manufacturing is often associated with automation, service sectors such as retail, hospitality, and customer support are also experiencing a significant shift. In these industries, automation is used to improve customer service, increase efficiency, and reduce costs. Many businesses are adopting automated systems that interact directly with customers, improving speed and satisfaction.

For instance, in retail, self-checkout kiosks and automated payment systems have become commonplace, allowing customers to complete their transactions without the need for a cashier. Similarly, virtual assistants and chatbots are now widely used in customer service, providing quick, 24/7 support for everything from answering questions to processing orders.

The Rise of Chatbots and AI in Customer Service

Chatbots are a prime example of how artificial intelligence (AI) is transforming customer service. By leveraging natural language processing (NLP), these automated systems can engage with customers, understand their requests, and provide solutions or direct them to the appropriate human representatives. For example, large corporations such as banks and telecom companies have implemented AI-driven chatbots to handle common customer inquiries like billing issues, technical problems, or account management. These systems can handle hundreds of inquiries simultaneously, significantly reducing wait times and freeing up human agents to address more complex issues.

In addition, AI is increasingly being used in the service sector for personalizing customer experiences. Automated recommendation systems used by platforms like Netflix and Amazon analyze consumer behavior and suggest products or content based on previous interactions. This personalized service has become an essential tool for increasing customer loyalty and sales.

Automation in Healthcare: Improving Accuracy and Efficiency

Healthcare is another industry where automation is making a profound impact. The use of robots and AI in healthcare is revolutionizing how procedures are performed, diagnoses are made, and patient care is delivered. One prominent example is robotic surgery. In robotic-assisted surgeries, surgeons use robotic arms controlled by computers to perform delicate procedures with greater precision and control than traditional methods. The da Vinci Surgical System, for example, enables surgeons to perform minimally invasive surgeries with improved accuracy, faster recovery times, and fewer complications.

In addition to surgery, automation is being used in administrative tasks within healthcare. Medical records, patient scheduling, and even billing are now often handled by automated systems, freeing up healthcare workers to focus on patient care.

Automation in Transportation and Logistics: Streamlining Operations

The transportation and logistics industries are also seeing widespread adoption of automation, particularly in warehousing and delivery operations. In warehouses, robots and automated systems are used to transport goods, pick orders, and organize inventory. Companies like Amazon have integrated sophisticated robotic systems into their fulfillment centers, where robots work alongside human workers to pick and pack products with incredible speed and efficiency.

Another area where automation is rapidly growing is in transportation. Autonomous vehicles, including trucks and drones, are poised to revolutionize the delivery process. Self-driving trucks are being tested to transport goods across long distances, reducing the need for human drivers and improving fuel efficiency. Similarly, drones are being used for last-mile delivery, where they can quickly transport small packages directly to consumers' homes.

The Hospitality Industry: Robots in Hotels and Restaurants

The hospitality industry has also embraced automation in an effort to improve efficiency and reduce labor costs. In hotels, automated check-in kiosks allow guests to check into their rooms without interacting with hotel staff, while robots are used to deliver room service and even clean rooms. Similarly, in restaurants, robots are being used for tasks like taking orders, serving food, and even cooking. Automated cooking systems can prepare meals consistently and efficiently, reducing the need for skilled labor and ensuring quality.

The Future of Automation in Service Sectors

The future of automation in service industries looks promising. As AI, machine learning, and robotics continue to advance, we can expect even more industries to adopt automated systems. Automation in the service sector will continue to evolve, with robots becoming more sophisticated in handling tasks that require human-like decision-making and emotional intelligence. However, while automation in the service sector can lead to improved efficiency, it also raises concerns about job displacement. As more tasks are automated, workers will need to adapt by learning new skills or transitioning to roles that cannot easily be automated.

The Growing Role of Automation in Other Industries

Automation is also making inroads in other sectors, such as finance, education, and construction. In finance, AI is being used for algorithmic trading, risk assessment, and fraud detection. In education, online learning platforms are employing automation to deliver personalized learning experiences to students. In construction, robotic systems are being used to build structures, laying bricks, welding, and even 3D-printing buildings.

Conclusion: Automation's Widespread Impact

The rise of automation in the workplace is reshaping industries across the globe. From manufacturing and healthcare to customer service and transportation, automated systems are improving efficiency, reducing costs, and enhancing the overall quality of work. However, as automation becomes more prevalent, businesses and workers must prepare for the inevitable changes it brings. In the next chapter, we will delve deeper into the challenges and opportunities that automation presents, particularly in terms of workforce displacement and the future of employment.

This chapter provides a comprehensive look at the rise of automation across various industries, highlighting real-world examples and its impact on different sectors. Let me know if you'd like any changes or additions!

CHAPTER 4

ROBOTICS IN INDUSTRY: PAST, PRESENT, AND FUTURE

Introduction to Robotics in Industry

Robotics has come a long way since its humble beginnings, transforming industries and revolutionizing the way tasks are performed. From early mechanical systems to advanced AI-powered robots, the role of robotics in industrial settings has continually expanded. In this chapter, we will explore the evolution of robotics in various industries, examine current applications, and discuss future trends that could reshape industrial work in the years to come.

The Birth of Industrial Robotics: Early Developments

The concept of robotics dates back to ancient times, but the industrial use of robots began in the mid-20th century. In the 1950s and 1960s, the first industrial robots were introduced, designed primarily for tasks in manufacturing environments. These early robots were quite basic, primarily performing repetitive actions such as welding, assembly, and material handling.

One of the first commercially successful industrial robots was Unimate, developed by George Devol and Joseph Engelberger in the 1950s. Unimate was installed in a General Motors factory in 1961 to perform tasks like lifting and placing parts onto an assembly line. Although primitive by today's standards, Unimate marked the beginning of robotics' integration into industrial operations.

The 1970s to 1990s: Expansion and Automation

As the decades passed, robots became more sophisticated and versatile, incorporating advances in computing, sensors, and programming. In the 1970s, the introduction of microprocessors allowed robots to become more programmable, enabling them to perform a wider range of tasks. By the 1980s, robots began to be used not just in manufacturing but also in industries such as electronics and food processing.

During this time, robots were primarily used for high-precision tasks in controlled environments, such as welding car parts or assembling electronic components. The main

31

benefits of robotics during this period were increased productivity, improved quality, and a reduction in human error.

Present-Day Robotics: Advanced Automation and AI Integration

Today, robotics has evolved far beyond its initial applications. Modern industrial robots are highly sophisticated machines capable of performing complex tasks with incredible precision and flexibility. The advent of AI, machine learning, and advanced sensors has led to the development of robots that can adapt to changing environments, make decisions, and work collaboratively with humans.

Collaborative Robots (Cobots)

One of the most significant advancements in the robotics industry is the development of collaborative robots, or "cobots." Unlike traditional robots, which typically isolated from human workers for safety reasons, cobots are designed to work alongside people. These robots are equipped with advanced sensors and AI systems that allow them to safely interact with humans, often in shared workspaces.

For example, in a manufacturing setting, cobots can assist human workers by performing repetitive tasks such as assembling components or lifting heavy objects, thus freeing up human workers to focus on more complex tasks. Collaborative robots are also being used in industries such as healthcare, where they assist in surgeries or help with patient care.

Autonomous Mobile Robots (AMRs)

Autonomous mobile robots (AMRs) are another key development in modern industrial robotics. Unlike traditional robots that are fixed in place, AMRs are mobile and can navigate through a workspace without human intervention. These robots are used in warehouses, distribution centers, and factories to transport materials, pick orders, and assist in inventory management.

AMRs are equipped with advanced navigation systems, such as LIDAR and computer vision, that allow them to understand their environment and make decisions in real-time. For example, in Amazon's fulfillment centers, AMRs transport goods from storage areas to packing stations, streamlining the order fulfillment process and reducing the need for human workers to perform these tasks.

Robots in Manufacturing: Precision and Speed

In today's manufacturing environments, robots are capable of performing an increasingly diverse range of tasks. Robots are used in industries like automotive, aerospace, electronics, and consumer goods manufacturing, where they excel at high-precision tasks such as welding, painting, and assembling parts.

In the automotive industry, robots are used to weld car bodies, install parts, and conduct inspections. For example, the Tesla factory relies heavily on robots to assemble its electric vehicles, ensuring that each car is built with speed and precision. In electronics manufacturing, robots are used to place tiny components onto circuit boards with micron-level accuracy.

Robotics in Healthcare: Revolutionizing Patient Care

Healthcare is another sector where robotics is having a profound impact. Robots are increasingly being used for surgeries, rehabilitation, and patient care. Robotic-assisted surgery systems, such as the da Vinci Surgical System, allow surgeons to perform minimally invasive surgeries with greater precision and smaller incisions, resulting in faster recovery times for patients.

Robots are also used in rehabilitation centers to help patients recover mobility after injuries. For example, robotic exoskeletons can assist patients with spinal cord injuries by allowing them to stand and walk, improving both their physical recovery and their psychological well-being.

Future Trends in Robotics: What's Next?

The future of robotics is filled with exciting possibilities. As technology continues to advance, we can expect robots to become even more integrated into industrial workflows, performing a wider variety of tasks with greater autonomy and intelligence.

Artificial Intelligence and Machine Learning

The integration of AI and machine learning will continue to drive innovation in robotics. Future robots will be able to "learn" from their environments, improving their performance over time and adapting to new tasks. This could lead to robots that can perform more complex, decision-

35

making tasks and interact with humans in more natural and intuitive ways.

Robotics as a Service (RaaS)

As robotics technology becomes more affordable and accessible, the concept of Robotics as a Service (RaaS) is gaining traction. In this model, companies can lease robotic systems on-demand rather than investing in expensive equipment upfront. This allows small and medium-sized businesses to integrate automation into their operations without the need for significant capital expenditure.

RaaS could significantly expand the reach of robotics, allowing companies across various industries to take advantage of automation without the financial burden of owning and maintaining robotic systems.

Robots in Construction: Building the Future

Robotics is also making its way into construction. Robots are being developed to assist in tasks like bricklaying, 3D printing buildings, and even constructing entire structures autonomously. For example, the construction company ICON has developed a 3D printer capable of building homes in a matter of days, using a special concrete-like material.

This technology could revolutionize housing construction, reducing costs and time required to build homes.

The Role of Robotics in Space Exploration

The exploration of space is another area where robotics is making significant strides. Robots are being used for tasks such as exploring distant planets, assembling satellites, and performing repairs in space. Robotic rovers, like NASA's Perseverance Rover, are collecting valuable data on Mars and sending it back to Earth, helping scientists better understand the planet's surface and its potential for supporting life.

Conclusion: A Future Shaped by Robotics

Robotics has come a long way since its early days in industrial applications. Today, robots are smarter, more flexible, and more capable than ever before. As AI, machine learning, and advanced sensors continue to evolve, the future of robotics looks even more promising. Industries will continue to adopt robots to improve efficiency, reduce costs, and enhance safety. However, with these advancements come challenges related to workforce displacement, skills gaps, and ethical considerations. Understanding the role of robotics in industry will be crucial for navigating the future of work in a world increasingly dominated by intelligent machines.

This chapter offers a comprehensive look at the history, present applications, and future trends of robotics in industry. Let me know if you'd like any modifications or deeper dives into specific examples!

CHAPTER 5

HOW AUTOMATION IS RESHAPING MANUFACTURING

Introduction: The Transformation of Manufacturing Through Automation

Manufacturing has always been a key driver of economic growth, and over the last several decades, it has undergone a dramatic transformation due to automation. Automation involves using technology, including machines, robots, and software, to perform tasks traditionally carried out by human workers. In this chapter, we will explore how automated systems are reshaping the manufacturing process, reducing the need for human labor in some areas, and improving efficiency, quality, and safety in others.

The Rise of Automated Systems in Manufacturing

Automation in manufacturing is not a recent phenomenon. It began with the introduction of mechanized systems in the 18th century during the Industrial Revolution. However, the true impact of automation was felt in the 20th century with the advent of computer-controlled machines and industrial robots. Early automation primarily involved repetitive tasks, such as assembly lines in car manufacturing, where the speed and precision of machines made them more efficient than human labor.

Today, automation goes far beyond simple mechanization. It encompasses everything from advanced robotics to artificial intelligence (AI) and machine learning (ML), which enable machines to handle tasks that were once too complex or nuanced for traditional automation.

Key Areas Where Automation is Reshaping Manufacturing

1. Assembly Lines and Robotics

The most visible change in manufacturing automation has occurred in assembly lines, where robots and machines have taken over repetitive tasks like assembly, welding, painting, and packaging. This allows manufacturers to produce goods more efficiently and with greater consistency.

For example, in the automotive industry, companies like Toyota and Tesla have adopted robotic systems for assembling car parts. Robots perform tasks such as welding car frames and installing windshields, reducing the need for human workers to engage in physically demanding tasks. These robots are highly accurate and can work continuously, increasing production speed and product quality while reducing errors.

2. Precision and Quality Control

Automation has also led to significant improvements in product quality. With automated systems, manufacturers can use advanced sensors and cameras to monitor products during production, ensuring that they meet the highest standards of precision.

In industries like electronics and pharmaceuticals, even the smallest error can result in costly mistakes. Automated quality control systems use sensors, cameras, and AI-powered algorithms to inspect products at every stage of production. This technology ensures that defects are caught early in the process, reducing the number of faulty products that make it to the end consumer.

For example, in the production of smartphones, automated systems scan for pixel defects in screens, ensuring that only flawless units are shipped out. In the food industry,

41

automated machines check for contamination, ensuring that products are safe and high quality.

3. Material Handling and Logistics

Automated material handling systems are another key component of modern manufacturing. These systems use robots and conveyors to move materials and finished products through the factory floor without human intervention. This reduces the risk of injury and increases the efficiency of warehouse operations.

In large manufacturing plants, robots called Automated Guided Vehicles (AGVs) are used to transport raw materials and finished goods between different parts of the factory. AGVs follow pre-programmed paths and are equipped with sensors to avoid obstacles and navigate through crowded environments. This allows manufacturers to improve workflow and reduce downtime, which is often caused by manual material handling.

4. Additive Manufacturing (3D Printing)

Additive manufacturing, commonly known as 3D printing, is another example of automation in the manufacturing process. Unlike traditional subtractive manufacturing, where material is cut away from a larger block, 3D printing builds objects layer by layer. This technology has revolutionized prototyping and production in industries like aerospace, automotive, and healthcare.

For instance, companies like GE and Airbus are using 3D printing to create complex, lightweight components for aircraft engines. These parts are stronger, more durable, and lighter than traditional metal parts, leading to better performance and reduced fuel consumption in airplanes.

Reducing Human Labor Through Automation

One of the most significant effects of automation in manufacturing is the reduction of human labor in certain tasks. As robots and automated systems take over repetitive, dangerous, or monotonous tasks, human workers are freed up to focus on more complex and creative aspects of the production process.

For example, while robots may handle tasks like assembling components or welding, human workers may oversee the machines, troubleshoot issues, or perform tasks that require human intuition, creativity, or problem-solving skills. In many cases, automation has led to the creation of new roles, such as robot programmers, maintenance technicians, and data analysts, which require specialized knowledge and expertise.

However, the automation of labor-intensive tasks has led to concerns about job displacement. In industries where human workers were previously responsible for tasks like manual assembly or packaging, automation has reduced the demand for such labor. As a result, workers in these industries may need to retrain or reskill to remain competitive in the job market.

Increasing Efficiency and Reducing Costs

One of the primary drivers behind the adoption of automation in manufacturing is the potential for increased efficiency and cost savings. Automated systems can work around the clock without taking breaks, leading to significant improvements in production speed and volume. Robots and machines can perform tasks with consistent precision, reducing the risk of human error and minimizing waste.

For example, automated inventory management systems allow manufacturers to track raw materials and finished goods in real time, preventing overstocking or shortages. In the long term, this leads to cost savings, as manufacturers can better manage resources and avoid production delays due to inventory issues.

In addition, automation helps manufacturers optimize their operations by collecting and analyzing data in real time. AI and machine learning algorithms can analyze this data to identify patterns, predict maintenance needs, and even optimize the production schedule. This predictive maintenance reduces downtime and extends the lifespan of machines, ultimately lowering maintenance costs.

Safety Improvements Through Automation

Automation has also improved safety in manufacturing environments. Dangerous tasks that were once performed by human workers, such as handling hazardous materials or working in high-risk environments, are now carried out by robots and automated systems. For example, robots are used in chemical plants to handle toxic substances or in mining operations to work in environments with high levels of dust or gases.

By removing humans from high-risk tasks, manufacturers can reduce the number of workplace accidents and improve employee safety. This shift has led to a significant reduction in worker injuries and fatalities in certain industries.

The Future of Automation in Manufacturing

Looking ahead, the role of automation in manufacturing will continue to grow. Advances in robotics, AI, and the Internet of Things (IoT) will lead to even smarter, more efficient systems that can make real-time decisions, self-optimize, and adapt to changing conditions. The future of manufacturing will be increasingly characterized by "smart factories," where machines communicate with each other and with human workers to create a more flexible, efficient, and adaptable production environment.

For example, 5G connectivity and IoT sensors will enable machines to send and receive data instantaneously, creating more synchronized production lines. Artificial intelligence will allow machines to not only perform tasks but also learn from past experiences and optimize their performance over time. Additionally, the use of cobots—robots that work side-by-side with human workers—will become more widespread, leading to greater collaboration between humans and machines.

Conclusion: A New Era of Manufacturing

Automation has already reshaped the manufacturing process in profound ways, reducing labor, increasing efficiency, improving safety, and cutting costs. As technology continues to evolve, the role of automation in manufacturing will only grow, leading to even greater levels of productivity and innovation. However, this transformation also raises important questions about the future of work and the need for workers to adapt to an increasingly automated world.

In the next chapter, we will explore how automation is affecting other industries beyond manufacturing and the broader implications it has for the global workforce.

This chapter provides a thorough examination of how automation is transforming manufacturing, from early advancements to future trends. Let me know if you'd like any adjustments or if you'd like to explore a particular aspect in more detail!

CHAPTER 6

ROBOTICS IN HEALTHCARE: TRANSFORMING PATIENT CARE

Introduction: The Role of Robotics in Healthcare

Healthcare is an industry where precision, safety, and efficiency are paramount. In recent years, robots have emerged as powerful tools, improving the quality of patient care, enhancing surgical outcomes, and streamlining administrative processes. From assisting in complex surgeries to providing elderly care, robots are revolutionizing the healthcare landscape. In this chapter, we will explore how robots are currently being used in healthcare, the benefits they offer, and the future potential of robotics in medicine.

The Evolution of Robotics in Healthcare

The integration of robotics into healthcare has progressed rapidly over the last few decades. Early robots in healthcare were used for simple tasks such as transporting medication, cleaning rooms, or moving equipment. However, with advances in artificial intelligence (AI), machine learning, and precision engineering, robots are now capable of performing highly complex and delicate medical procedures, contributing to better patient outcomes and reduced risks.

The first robotic surgery systems were introduced in the 1980s, but it wasn't until the 2000s that the technology became widely adopted in operating rooms. Today, robots assist in surgeries, rehabilitation, patient monitoring, and a variety of other medical applications, helping healthcare professionals provide higher levels of care with greater efficiency.

Robots in Surgery: Precision and Minimally Invasive Procedures

One of the most groundbreaking applications of robotics in healthcare is in the field of surgery. Robotic-assisted surgery allows surgeons to perform delicate and complex procedures with enhanced precision and control, often through smaller incisions. This leads to quicker recovery times, reduced risk of complications, and less pain for patients.

The **da Vinci Surgical System**, for example, is one of the most widely used robotic platforms for minimally invasive surgery. It features a robotic arm that is controlled by the surgeon, providing superior dexterity, vision, and precision compared to traditional manual surgery. Surgeons can perform procedures such as prostatectomies, heart valve repairs, and gynecological surgeries with greater accuracy, reducing the need for large incisions and enabling faster recovery times for patients.

Another major advancement in robotic surgery is the use of **robotic endoscopes**. These robots can navigate the human body in ways that were previously impossible, allowing surgeons to perform procedures such as biopsies or remove tumors with minimal disruption to surrounding tissue. Endoscopic surgery is often preferred because it reduces the risk of infection, scarring, and recovery time.

Robots in Patient Care: Enhancing Quality of Life

In addition to surgery, robots are making significant contributions to patient care, particularly in areas such as elderly care, rehabilitation, and mental health.

1. **Elderly Care and Assistance**

With the aging population in many parts of the world, there is an increasing demand for caregiving services. Robots are being developed to assist elderly patients with mobility, medication management, and daily tasks. These robots not only help improve the quality of life for patients but also reduce the burden on human caregivers.

For example, **assistive robots** like **PARO**, a therapeutic robot designed to resemble a baby seal, have been used in nursing homes to provide comfort and companionship to elderly patients. PARO interacts with patients by responding to touch and sound, offering emotional support and helping reduce feelings of loneliness and depression.

Additionally, robots such as **TUG** are used in hospitals to transport supplies, medicine, and even food to patients, allowing healthcare staff to focus on more critical tasks. This kind of automation in patient care environments helps improve operational efficiency and patient satisfaction.

2. **Rehabilitation Robotics**

Rehabilitation robots are increasingly being used to help patients recover from injuries or surgery. These robots assist patients with physical therapy exercises by providing precise movements that encourage proper rehabilitation, enhancing recovery time and improving overall outcomes.

51

One such example is the **ReWalk exoskeleton**, a wearable robotic device that helps people with spinal cord injuries walk again. It supports the user's movements by providing powered hip and knee motion, allowing the user to stand up, walk, and even climb stairs. Such exoskeletons are a huge breakthrough for patients with mobility impairments and are transforming the field of physical rehabilitation.

Additionally, robots like **EksoGT** help patients recovering from strokes or brain injuries to regain mobility through repetitive, guided movements that stimulate neural recovery. These robots provide a consistent level of rehabilitation that human therapists may not be able to offer, helping patients achieve faster and more efficient results.

Robots in Diagnostics: Improving Accuracy and Speed

Robots are also making strides in medical diagnostics. In fields such as radiology, pathology, and oncology, robots assist doctors by analyzing data, identifying abnormalities, and providing more accurate diagnoses.

For instance, AI-powered robots are used to **analyze medical images**. Using deep learning algorithms, these robots can detect and identify early signs of diseases such as cancer, often with greater accuracy than human doctors. In some cases, robots are able to detect patterns in medical images that may be too subtle for the human eye to catch.

In pathology, robots are used to analyze tissue samples for signs of disease, reducing the time it takes to deliver results and improving the accuracy of diagnoses. In one example, **Pathology Robotics** helps streamline the workflow in laboratories, allowing automated systems to prepare, label, and analyze samples with minimal human intervention.

Robots in Mental Health Care: Supporting Therapy and Wellness

Robots are also being used to help improve mental health and wellness. AI-powered chatbots like **Woebot** are providing online support to people dealing with mental health issues, such as anxiety and depression. These chatbots use natural language processing (NLP) to engage in therapeutic conversations with users, offering cognitive-behavioral therapy (CBT) techniques and emotional support.

Another example is **Jibo**, a social robot designed to improve emotional well-being by engaging in friendly conversation with patients, especially elderly individuals or those in long-term care facilities. Jibo helps reduce feelings of loneliness by providing social interaction, making it a valuable tool in mental health care for isolated individuals.

The Future of Robotics in Healthcare

Looking ahead, robotics is expected to play an even larger role in transforming healthcare. As technology advances, robots will become more autonomous, intelligent, and integrated into the medical field.

1. **AI and Machine Learning in Robotics**

The integration of AI and machine learning will enable robots to learn from interactions with patients and medical professionals. This will allow robots to adapt to new environments, offer personalized patient care, and even make decisions in real-time to improve outcomes.

For instance, robots may one day be able to autonomously perform surgeries without direct human intervention, analyzing the patient's medical history, current condition, and surgical needs to determine the best course of action.

2. **Robotic Home Care and Telemedicine**

With the growing demand for home-based healthcare, robots will increasingly be used to provide care in patients' homes. Home robots could assist elderly patients by helping them move, taking their vital signs, administering medications, and providing companionship.

Additionally, **telemedicine** and robotic systems will make it easier for doctors to remotely monitor patients, conduct virtual consultations, and even guide robots to perform minor surgeries or diagnostic procedures from afar.

Challenges and Ethical Considerations

While the benefits of robotics in healthcare are clear, there are challenges and ethical considerations that need to be addressed. Privacy concerns, data security, and the potential for job displacement in healthcare professions are all issues that must be carefully managed as robots become more integrated into the healthcare system.

Additionally, the question of how much autonomy robots should have in medical decision-making is a critical issue. As robots become more capable, healthcare providers will need to strike a balance between leveraging technology and maintaining human oversight to ensure the best outcomes for patients.

Conclusion: The Promise of Robotics in Healthcare

Robots are already transforming healthcare in profound ways, from improving surgical outcomes to assisting with patient care and rehabilitation. As technology continues to evolve, robots will play an even more significant role in reshaping the healthcare industry, offering new opportunities for better care, enhanced precision, and improved quality of life for patients. However, the path forward will require careful consideration of ethical, legal, and social implications to ensure that robots are used responsibly and effectively in healthcare.

This chapter provides a detailed look at how robots are being used in healthcare today, with examples of current applications and a glimpse into what the future holds. Let me know if you'd like to explore any particular aspect further or if you have additional insights to incorporate!

CHAPTER 7

THE ROLE OF AI IN AUTOMATION AND ROBOTICS

Introduction: The Intersection of AI and Robotics

Artificial Intelligence (AI) and robotics have revolutionized many industries by bringing together machine learning, data processing, and automation technologies. While robotics focuses on designing machines capable of performing physical tasks, AI equips these machines with the ability to think, learn, and adapt to their environment. This chapter will break down the relationship between AI and robotics, illustrating how AI powers intelligent automation in various industries, transforming everything from manufacturing and healthcare to logistics and customer service.

What is Artificial Intelligence (AI)?

Artificial Intelligence refers to the ability of a machine to mimic human intelligence. This includes learning from experience, adapting to new situations, understanding natural language, and making decisions. AI systems use algorithms to process vast amounts of data and make predictions or decisions based on that data. The most common types of AI include machine learning (ML), natural language processing (NLP), and computer vision. These AI technologies allow machines to process information and perform tasks autonomously, which is key to their integration with robotics.

In robotics, AI allows robots to go beyond simple programmed tasks and perform complex actions. Robots powered by AI are capable of making real-time decisions, learning from their experiences, and interacting with humans or their environments in a more natural and efficient manner.

How AI Powers Robotics in Automation

AI has a profound impact on the effectiveness and capabilities of robots across industries. By enabling robots to perceive, analyze, and learn from their surroundings, AI enhances their flexibility and autonomy, making them more effective in performing tasks traditionally carried out by humans.

1. **Machine Learning and Robotics: Improving Performance Over Time**

One of the primary ways AI enhances robotics is through machine learning, which enables robots to learn from data and improve their performance over time. Through continuous exposure to different scenarios and data inputs, robots become more proficient in completing their tasks. Machine learning allows robots to identify patterns, optimize their actions, and adjust to new or unforeseen situations.

For example, in manufacturing, AI-powered robots used in quality control can learn from previous inspection data to identify defective products more accurately. With each production cycle, the system's ability to detect defects improves, reducing waste and increasing efficiency.

2. Computer Vision: Enabling Robots to See and Understand Their Environment

Computer vision is another key area where AI has a direct impact on robotics. Through computer vision, robots can analyze visual information from their surroundings, such as images or video feeds, and use that data to make informed decisions. AI algorithms enable robots to recognize objects, track movement, and navigate spaces by processing visual data in real time.

In manufacturing, for instance, robots equipped with computer vision can inspect parts for defects during production. In the healthcare industry, robotic surgery systems use computer vision to view and analyze patients' organs in high resolution, allowing surgeons to perform precise and minimally invasive operations.

3. **Natural Language Processing (NLP): Enabling Robots to Understand and Interact with Humans**

Natural language processing (NLP) is an AI technology that allows robots to understand and respond to human language. NLP enables robots to interpret spoken commands, ask questions, and provide verbal feedback. This makes it possible for robots to interact with humans more naturally, enhancing human-robot collaboration.

In industries like customer service, AI-powered chatbots are increasingly used to interact with customers, answering their inquiries and resolving issues. In healthcare, robots like **PARO**, a therapeutic robot used for elderly patients, can communicate with patients through basic vocalizations, providing companionship and emotional support.

Applications of AI-Powered Robotics in Various Industries

1. Manufacturing: Automating Complex Tasks and Improving Efficiency

AI-powered robots have had a transformative impact on the manufacturing industry, automating complex tasks that were previously impossible or too expensive to automate. AI enables robots to learn from production data and adapt to changes in the manufacturing environment.

For instance, in **automated assembly lines**, robots equipped with AI can adjust their actions in response to changes in product designs, material variations, or machine malfunctions. AI allows these robots to optimize their movements, increasing production speed while maintaining high-quality standards.

Additionally, AI-powered robots are used in predictive maintenance, where they analyze data from sensors to predict when a machine might break down. This reduces downtime and ensures that equipment runs smoothly, saving time and costs associated with unplanned repairs.

2. Healthcare: Robotic Surgery and Patient Care

In the healthcare industry, AI plays a crucial role in improving the precision and capabilities of robotic systems. **Robotic surgery systems**, such as the da Vinci Surgical System, combine robotics with AI to assist surgeons in performing complex procedures with enhanced accuracy and minimal invasiveness. AI allows the system to analyze the patient's anatomy in real-time, enabling the robot to make adjustments and provide support for the surgeon during surgery.

AI is also transforming patient care. Robots like **TUG** are used in hospitals to transport medical supplies, medicine, and food, improving efficiency in healthcare delivery. AI allows these robots to navigate hospitals autonomously, avoiding obstacles and following designated routes to deliver essential items.

3. **Logistics and Supply Chain: Optimizing Operations with AI Robots**

AI-powered robots are increasingly being deployed in logistics and supply chain management to streamline operations. In warehouses, robots such as **AMRs (Autonomous Mobile Robots)** use AI to navigate through aisles, pick and transport goods, and ensure that products are delivered to the correct locations. By learning from previous routes, these robots optimize their paths to reduce travel time and increase efficiency.

AI also plays a role in **inventory management**. Robots equipped with AI can track product levels, monitor stock movements, and identify discrepancies in inventory. This reduces human error and helps companies maintain a more accurate and efficient inventory system.

4. Customer Service: Enhancing Interaction with AI-Powered Robots

Customer service is one area where AI and robotics have made significant strides. AI-powered robots are increasingly being used to assist customers with tasks such as answering questions, processing transactions, and providing recommendations.

For instance, **chatbots** and **virtual assistants** powered by AI help businesses offer around-the-clock support to customers, addressing inquiries related to product information, order status, and troubleshooting. In physical stores, robots equipped with AI can assist customers by providing directions, answering product-related questions, and even guiding them through the checkout process.

5. Agriculture: AI and Robotics for Precision Farming

In agriculture, AI-powered robots are improving efficiency by performing tasks such as planting, harvesting, and monitoring crop health. AI enables robots to analyze soil conditions, weather patterns, and crop growth, making it possible to optimize planting schedules and irrigation systems.

For example, robots like **Octinion's Rubion** use AI to detect ripe fruit and harvest it without damaging the crop. This ensures that only the best produce is collected, leading to higher yields and reduced waste.

Future Trends: AI and Robotics Integration

As AI and robotics continue to advance, the potential applications will expand. In the future, AI-powered robots will become more autonomous, able to operate in dynamic environments with little to no human intervention. Here are a few possible trends:

- **Collaborative Robots (Cobots):** Cobots, which are designed to work alongside human workers, will become more common in industries like manufacturing and healthcare. These robots will be able to understand human gestures and emotions, improving human-robot collaboration.

- **Autonomous Robotics:** Robots will be able to operate in more complex and unpredictable environments, such as disaster zones, underwater, or outer space, making real-time decisions based on sensory data.

- **AI and Human-Machine Interfaces:** AI will continue to improve how robots interact with humans, with intuitive interfaces such as voice recognition, gesture control, and even brain-computer interfaces (BCIs), allowing for more seamless collaboration.

Conclusion: The Symbiotic Relationship Between AI and Robotics

AI and robotics are two technologies that complement each other perfectly, with AI bringing intelligence and decision-making capabilities to robotic systems. Together, they have the potential to revolutionize industries by automating tasks, improving efficiency, and enhancing human capabilities. As these technologies continue to evolve, their impact on the workforce and society at large will only grow, making it essential to understand the role of AI in shaping the future of automation and robotics.

This chapter provides an in-depth exploration of how AI powers robotics and the intelligent automation of various industries. Let me know if you'd like to expand on any section or add more specific examples!

CHAPTER 8

AUTOMATION IN RETAIL: THE CHANGING FACE OF SHOPPING

Introduction: The Rise of Automation in Retail

The retail industry has been transformed over the years by automation, with new technologies reshaping how products are sold, stored, and delivered. From cashierless stores and self-checkout systems to automated warehouses and AI-driven inventory management, automation is making retail faster, more efficient, and more customer-centric. In this chapter, we will explore how automation is affecting retail operations, examining the changes it has brought to the shopping experience and the ways retailers are adapting to meet evolving consumer expectations.

The Advent of Automation in Retail: From the Past to the Present

Automation in retail has been a gradual but continuous process. Early forms of automation were seen in the introduction of conveyor belts in warehouses and simple barcode scanners at checkout counters. However, in recent years, we've seen a dramatic acceleration in the adoption of advanced technologies that offer not just operational efficiency but also a fundamental shift in how customers interact with stores and products.

Self-Checkout and Cashierless Stores: The Evolution of the Checkout Process

One of the most visible impacts of automation in retail is in the checkout process. Self-checkout machines have been a game changer in speeding up transactions and reducing the need for human cashiers. Customers can scan their items, pay via credit/debit cards, mobile wallets, or even contactless methods, and be on their way in just a few minutes. These systems have grown increasingly user-friendly, allowing stores to reduce labor costs while enhancing the overall customer experience.

A more advanced form of this is the concept of **cashierless stores**, where the entire checkout process is automated. One of the most famous examples of this innovation is **Amazon Go**, which uses a combination of AI, sensors, and computer vision to track the items customers pick up as they walk through the store. Shoppers simply enter the store, pick up the items they want, and leave. The system automatically charges them via their Amazon account, and there is no need for a traditional checkout process.

This technology is expanding rapidly, with many other retail chains adopting similar models. Cashierless stores eliminate the wait times typically associated with checkout lines and create a frictionless shopping experience that appeals to busy consumers looking for convenience.

AI-Driven Personalization: Enhancing the Shopping Experience

AI has significantly enhanced the personalization of the shopping experience, allowing retailers to offer more tailored services and product recommendations. Retailers use AI algorithms to track customers' browsing habits, preferences, and past purchases to suggest products that are more likely to resonate with individual shoppers.

For example, e-commerce giants like Amazon and Walmart use AI-powered recommendation engines that suggest products based on customer behavior, enhancing the likelihood of additional purchases. In brick-and-mortar stores, AI-driven tools help sales associates provide personalized recommendations in real time, based on a customer's preferences or purchase history.

Moreover, AI helps optimize pricing strategies. Dynamic pricing algorithms adjust the price of products based on demand, competitor prices, time of day, or even the customer's location, allowing retailers to maximize profits and remain competitive.

Automated Warehouses: Revolutionizing Inventory Management and Order Fulfillment

In addition to transforming the shopping experience itself, automation is also reshaping how products are stored and delivered. **Automated warehouses** use robots, drones, and AI systems to handle the movement of goods, from receiving and sorting items to picking and packing orders for delivery. This significantly reduces human error, accelerates the process, and enhances accuracy.

For instance, **Amazon Robotics**, formerly known as Kiva Systems, has revolutionized Amazon's warehouse operations by using autonomous robots to transport goods to human workers, who then pack and ship the items. These robots navigate the warehouse floor using sensors and algorithms, improving efficiency and reducing the need for human labor in tasks such as retrieving products from shelves.

Another example is **Ocado**, a UK-based online grocery retailer, which employs robots and AI to manage inventory and fulfill orders in its highly automated fulfillment centers. Ocado's system uses robotic arms and automated systems to ensure that groceries are picked and packed quickly, allowing the company to offer faster delivery times to customers.

The benefits of automated warehouses include increased operational speed, reduced costs, and improved order accuracy. By integrating AI and robotics, retailers can meet growing customer demands for faster shipping and more efficient inventory management.

Robotic Process Automation (RPA) in Retail Operations

In addition to physical automation in stores and warehouses, many retailers are leveraging **Robotic Process Automation (RPA)** in their back-office operations. RPA uses software robots to automate repetitive tasks such as inventory tracking, order processing, payroll, and customer service inquiries.

For instance, RPA is being used to automate inventory management by automatically tracking stock levels and placing orders when supplies run low. In the customer service department, RPA is employed to answer common customer queries via chatbots, ensuring that customers receive instant assistance without the need for human intervention.

By automating back-office processes, retailers can reduce administrative overhead, free up human resources for higher-value tasks, and improve operational efficiency.

The Future of Shopping: Augmented Reality (AR) and Virtual Try-Ons

As technology continues to evolve, **Augmented Reality (AR)** is playing an increasingly important role in retail, especially in e-commerce. AR allows customers to virtually try on products before purchasing, whether it's clothing, makeup, or even furniture. This immersive shopping experience reduces uncertainty and enhances customer satisfaction.

For example, **L'Oreal** has developed AR-enabled makeup apps that allow customers to try on different products virtually using their smartphones, providing a personalized shopping experience. Similarly, furniture stores like **IKEA** use AR to help customers visualize how furniture pieces will look in their own homes by overlaying digital models of the items onto a live view of their living space through their mobile devices.

This technology provides a significant advantage by helping customers make informed decisions before purchasing, leading to higher conversion rates and fewer returns.

The Role of Robots in Customer Service and Store Operations

Robots are also being deployed in retail stores to assist customers and perform operational tasks. **Service robots** like **Pepper**, a humanoid robot, are used in retail environments to greet customers, provide store information, and even engage in basic conversation. These robots are equipped with AI and can adapt to customer behavior, making interactions feel more personal.

In addition to enhancing customer engagement, robots are also being used in-store for tasks like cleaning, shelf scanning, and inventory management. For instance, Walmart has deployed robots in its stores to scan shelves, check for missing items, and even clean floors. This allows employees to focus on more valuable tasks, such as customer service and restocking shelves.

The Impact of Automation on Retail Jobs

While automation in retail brings many benefits, it also raises questions about the future of retail jobs. Automation technologies, such as cashierless stores, robotic warehouse operations, and AI-driven customer service, have the potential to displace certain types of jobs, particularly in roles that involve repetitive tasks.

However, automation also creates new job opportunities. As retailers adopt more advanced technologies, there is an increasing demand for skilled workers in fields such as robotics, AI programming, data analytics, and customer experience management. Moreover, automation allows retail workers to focus on more complex and creative tasks, such as enhancing customer service, driving sales, and managing product innovation.

Conclusion: A New Era for Retail

Automation is reshaping the retail landscape, making shopping faster, more personalized, and more efficient. From cashierless stores and AI-driven customer service to automated warehouses and AR try-ons, technology is transforming every aspect of the retail experience. While these innovations bring significant benefits for consumers and retailers alike, they also require a new approach to workforce training and job development.

As we move forward, it is clear that automation will continue to shape the future of retail. Retailers who embrace these technological changes and use them to enhance the customer experience will be well-positioned to thrive in the ever-evolving retail environment.

This chapter highlights the transformative role of automation in the retail industry, exploring the various technologies that are reshaping how consumers shop and how retailers operate. Let me know if you'd like any further elaboration on specific sections or additional examples!

CHAPTER 9

THE FUTURE OF WORK IN AGRICULTURE

Introduction: Revolutionizing Agriculture with Robotics and Automation

Agriculture has always been the backbone of human civilization, but over the centuries, it has undergone numerous transformations, especially with the introduction of new technologies. Today, robotics and automation are poised to lead the next wave of innovation in farming, dramatically altering how food is grown, harvested, and distributed. From autonomous tractors and drones to precision farming technologies, robots are increasingly being used to enhance productivity, reduce labor costs, and improve sustainability in agriculture. In this chapter, we will explore how these technologies are reshaping the agricultural landscape and what the future holds for workers in this vital sector.

The Rise of Robotics and Automation in Agriculture

Agricultural robotics and automation began with mechanization in the early 20th century. Tractors, harvesters, and plows replaced manual labor, increasing the efficiency of farming operations. However, modern robotics and automation represent a quantum leap in this evolution, offering farmers the ability to monitor and manage their farms in ways that were previously unimaginable.

Today's agricultural robots combine cutting-edge AI, GPS, and sensor technology to perform tasks that are more precise, efficient, and sustainable. These technologies allow for the optimization of every stage of farming, from planting seeds to harvesting crops, monitoring soil health, and managing pests.

Autonomous Tractors: Driving the Future of Fieldwork

One of the most notable advancements in agricultural robotics is the development of **autonomous tractors**. These self-driving tractors are designed to perform the heavy lifting in fields, replacing traditional manual labor and increasing efficiency. Powered by GPS and advanced sensors, autonomous tractors can navigate fields on their own, performing tasks like plowing, sowing, and fertilizing with minimal human intervention.

For example, **Case IH** and **John Deere**, two of the world's leading agricultural equipment manufacturers, have introduced autonomous tractors that can operate 24/7, significantly increasing productivity. These machines use real-time data from GPS systems, soil sensors, and weather forecasts to adjust their operations based on field conditions, ensuring that crops are planted at optimal depths, spacing, and timing.

The benefits of autonomous tractors extend beyond efficiency. By automating tasks that are physically demanding, these machines can help reduce the risk of injury and minimize human labor on the farm, allowing workers to focus on more strategic tasks such as data analysis and decision-making.

Robotic Harvesters: Precision and Efficiency in Crop Collection

Robotic harvesters are another game-changer in modern agriculture. These robots are designed to autonomously pick crops with precision, reducing waste and minimizing damage to plants. They can operate in a variety of settings, from picking fruits and vegetables in orchards to harvesting grains in fields.

For example, **FFRobotics**, a robotics company, has developed a robot capable of harvesting apples with exceptional precision. The robot uses AI and advanced vision systems to identify ripe apples and pick them without bruising or damaging the fruit, which is a common problem in manual harvesting. This is particularly important for crops that require delicate handling, such as berries or tomatoes, where traditional harvesting methods can cause significant losses.

Similarly, **Agrobot**, a company focused on robotic strawberry harvesting, uses machine vision and AI to identify ripe strawberries and gently harvest them. This technology not only increases harvesting efficiency but also reduces labor costs, which can be a major expense for farmers, especially in labor-intensive crops.

Drones: Revolutionizing Monitoring and Data Collection

Drones are increasingly being used in agriculture to monitor crop health, assess field conditions, and optimize the use of resources. Equipped with high-resolution cameras and sensors, drones can capture aerial imagery of farmland, providing farmers with detailed insights into the health of their crops. These drones can monitor plant growth, detect pest infestations, and identify areas that require irrigation or fertilization.

PrecisionHawk, a drone technology company, provides farmers with aerial imagery that helps them track the health of their crops in real-time. By using multispectral and thermal sensors, drones can detect early signs of disease or nutrient deficiencies that may not be visible to the naked eye. With this data, farmers can take preventive actions to address issues before they affect the entire crop, improving yield and reducing the need for pesticides or fertilizers.

Drones are also used to map fields and generate 3D models, which helps farmers plan irrigation systems, analyze soil health, and optimize crop rotation. The ability to gather such detailed data allows for more precise management of agricultural resources, leading to increased efficiency and sustainability.

Robotic Weed Control: Reducing the Need for Chemicals

Weed control is one of the most labor-intensive and resource-heavy tasks in farming. Traditionally, farmers have relied on chemical herbicides to manage weeds, which can have negative environmental impacts. However, robotic systems are now being developed to perform **precision weed control** without the need for chemicals.

For instance, **The Tertill**, a solar-powered robot, is designed to autonomously weed vegetable gardens. It uses sensors to detect and remove weeds while leaving the crops intact. Similarly, **Ripe Robotics** is developing robots that can identify and remove weeds from crops, reducing the need for chemical herbicides and promoting sustainable farming practices.

This shift toward robotic weed control could lead to more environmentally friendly farming practices and significantly reduce the costs associated with herbicide application, both in terms of purchasing chemicals and labor.

Precision Farming: Data-Driven Agriculture for Maximum Efficiency

One of the most powerful applications of automation in agriculture is **precision farming**, which uses data and technology to make farming more efficient, sustainable, and productive. By combining sensors, drones, AI, and other technologies, farmers can monitor every aspect of their fields, from soil moisture and temperature to nutrient levels and crop health.

Precision agriculture systems can provide farmers with real-time data on crop conditions, allowing them to make informed decisions about irrigation, fertilization, pest control, and harvest timing. For example, soil moisture sensors connected to AI-powered systems can automatically activate irrigation systems, ensuring that crops receive the optimal amount of water.

This data-driven approach reduces waste, increases yields, and minimizes the environmental impact of farming. By using automation to monitor and manage resources more efficiently, precision farming helps farmers grow more food while conserving water, reducing chemical usage, and minimizing land degradation.

The Impact of Automation on the Agricultural Workforce

As automation continues to transform farming, it is clear that some tasks traditionally performed by human workers will be replaced by robots. Autonomous tractors, robotic harvesters, and drones can perform many of the labor-intensive tasks that were once handled by farmworkers. While this shift may reduce the demand for manual labor in certain areas, it also opens up new opportunities in areas like robotics maintenance, data analysis, and farm management.

Farmers and workers in the agricultural sector will need to adapt to this new landscape by acquiring skills in technology, data management, and robotics. This may require significant investments in education and training, but it also offers the potential for more rewarding and less physically demanding jobs in agriculture.

The Future of Agriculture: Automation, Sustainability, and Innovation

Looking ahead, the role of automation in agriculture is only set to grow. The next frontier in agricultural robotics will likely involve even greater integration of AI, robotics, and data analytics. This will allow farmers to create fully automated, smart farms where machines can autonomously handle planting, monitoring, harvesting, and even decision-making.

Moreover, as the global population continues to rise, automation will play a crucial role in ensuring food security.

By increasing productivity and reducing the environmental impact of farming, robotics and automation will be key to meeting the growing demand for food while protecting natural resources.

Conclusion: A New Era in Agriculture

The future of work in agriculture is one of innovation, sustainability, and increased efficiency. Robotics and automation are revolutionizing how farming is done, offering new possibilities for precision, productivity, and environmental responsibility. As these technologies continue to evolve, they will reshape the workforce in agriculture, creating new opportunities for workers to engage in more advanced roles while minimizing the need for labor in physically demanding tasks. For farmers, embracing automation will be essential for staying competitive in an increasingly technology-driven world.

This chapter explores how robotics and automation are transforming the agriculture industry, offering a glimpse into the future of farming. Let me know if you'd like to adjust any part of the chapter or explore additional technologies!

CHAPTER 10

THE IMPACT OF AUTOMATION ON THE SERVICE INDUSTRY

Introduction: Automation's Transformative Influence on Service Jobs

The service industry, one of the largest sectors of the global economy, is undergoing a profound transformation thanks to automation. From customer service to hospitality and transportation, automation technologies such as AI, robotics, and machine learning are redefining how service jobs are performed, changing both the experience for consumers and the responsibilities of workers. This chapter will examine how automation is reshaping service jobs across these industries and explore the benefits, challenges, and future implications for workers and businesses.

The Rise of Automation in the Service Industry

Historically, the service industry has been characterized by human interaction. Whether it's a hotel receptionist welcoming guests, a taxi driver transporting passengers, or a customer service representative assisting a client, human presence has been integral to these jobs. However, as technological advancements continue to unfold, the role of automation in service jobs has increased, particularly in routine, repetitive, or transactional tasks.

AI, robotics, and automated systems are increasingly taking on tasks such as answering customer inquiries, processing transactions, managing bookings, and even performing physical tasks like delivering food or cleaning. These technologies not only improve efficiency but also reduce operational costs and enhance customer satisfaction, all while pushing the boundaries of what automation can do in the service sector.

Customer Service: The Rise of Chatbots, Virtual Assistants, and AI

One of the most significant impacts of automation in the service industry is in **customer service**. Automation has revolutionized how businesses interact with customers, leading to the rise of AI-powered chatbots and virtual assistants. These tools can handle a wide range of customer interactions, providing support 24/7 and solving issues more efficiently than human agents.

Chatbots are now commonly used by companies to handle customer inquiries, process basic requests, and even resolve complaints. These AI-driven systems can interpret natural language, making them capable of answering questions, troubleshooting problems, and guiding customers through processes like password resets or product returns. Companies like **Zendesk**, **Intercom**, and **Drift** are using advanced chatbots to provide instant support, allowing customers to get answers without waiting in long queues or needing to speak to a human agent.

Beyond chatbots, **virtual assistants** like **Amazon's Alexa**, **Google Assistant**, and **Apple's Siri** are becoming more integrated into customer service platforms, enabling customers to interact with businesses through voice commands. These assistants can help customers make reservations, check product availability, place orders, and even make payments, offering a seamless and efficient customer experience.

While automation in customer service is effective for handling routine inquiries, there remains a need for human agents in more complex situations. However, automation has shifted the focus of customer service jobs. Human workers now tend to focus on higher-value tasks, such as solving complex issues, providing emotional support, and handling sensitive customer concerns.

Hospitality: Robots and Automation Changing the Guest Experience

The hospitality industry has seen one of the most notable shifts due to automation, as technology begins to take over routine tasks and redefine the customer experience. From check-in to room service, robots and automated systems are increasingly handling services traditionally provided by hotel staff.

Self-check-in kiosks are now a common feature in many hotels, enabling guests to check in and receive room keys without interacting with a receptionist. This not only speeds up the check-in process but also reduces the need for human staff to perform repetitive administrative tasks. Similarly, **robotic concierge services** are helping guests with requests like booking tickets, making dinner reservations, and recommending local attractions. Robots like **Connie**, developed by Hilton, are capable of providing hotel guests with information about the property, the local area, and amenities.

In **room service**, robots like **Relay**, designed by Savioke, can autonomously deliver food, beverages, and toiletries to hotel rooms. These robots navigate hotel hallways, use elevators, and even communicate with guests via touchscreen interfaces, providing a touchless, efficient experience.

Robotic cleaning systems, such as the **automated floor scrubbers** and **robotic vacuum cleaners**, are also becoming common in hospitality settings. These robots reduce the need for human cleaners and ensure that common areas, such as hotel lobbies and corridors, are consistently clean, improving operational efficiency while maintaining a high level of service.

While automation in hospitality helps reduce labor costs and improves service efficiency, it also changes the nature of jobs within the industry. Some roles, like front desk clerks or room service attendants, are being reduced, but new opportunities are emerging in areas such as robotics maintenance, system management, and customer experience design.

Transportation: The Emergence of Autonomous Vehicles and Drones

The transportation industry is undergoing a significant shift due to automation technologies, particularly **autonomous vehicles** and **delivery drones**. These advancements promise to increase efficiency, reduce costs, and change the workforce in the sector.

Self-driving cars and **autonomous trucks** are already being tested and, in some cases, deployed for transporting goods and passengers. Companies like **Waymo**, **Uber**, and **Tesla** are at the forefront of developing autonomous driving technology. These vehicles are equipped with AI, sensors, and machine learning systems that allow them to navigate roads, avoid obstacles, and make real-time decisions without human input. Autonomous trucks are expected to significantly reduce the need for long-haul truck drivers, but they also present opportunities for workers in tech-related roles, such as driving software development, machine learning, and vehicle maintenance.

Delivery drones are another example of automation transforming transportation. Companies like **Amazon** and **Wing**, a subsidiary of Alphabet, are developing drones for delivering small packages to customers quickly and efficiently. These drones use AI and GPS to navigate to customer locations, providing faster delivery times and

90

reducing the reliance on traditional delivery methods. As this technology becomes more widespread, it may reduce the demand for human delivery drivers, but also open up opportunities for workers in drone management, programming, and maintenance.

Automation's Impact on Employment in the Service Industry

While automation brings numerous benefits to service industries, it also raises important questions about employment. As robots and AI systems take over tasks like customer interaction, room service, and transportation, many jobs are at risk of displacement. Customer service representatives, hotel front desk clerks, and taxi drivers are among those whose roles may be affected by automation.

However, automation does not necessarily mean job loss across the board. Instead, it shifts the nature of employment within the service industry. As repetitive, manual tasks are automated, workers are increasingly required to possess skills in technology, data management, and customer relationship management. New roles are emerging that focus on overseeing automated systems, troubleshooting issues, and maintaining the infrastructure that supports these technologies.

Moreover, automation in service industries allows workers to focus on tasks that require emotional intelligence, creative problem-solving, and complex decision-making. For example, instead of answering routine customer questions, human agents can focus on delivering personalized service or handling complex cases that require empathy and understanding.

The Future of Automation in Service Industries

Looking ahead, the impact of automation on the service industry will only continue to grow. Future developments may include **smarter AI systems** capable of handling increasingly complex customer interactions, **robotic assistants** that provide more personalized services, and **autonomous delivery systems** that drastically cut down delivery times.

As these technologies continue to evolve, the service industry will increasingly rely on a hybrid workforce, where automation handles routine tasks and human workers focus on tasks requiring human ingenuity, empathy, and creativity.

Conclusion: A New Paradigm for Service Jobs

The impact of automation on the service industry is profound, transforming jobs and redefining the customer experience. While automation improves efficiency, reduces costs, and enhances service delivery, it also brings challenges regarding job displacement and workforce adaptation. However, as new technologies emerge, there will be new opportunities for workers with the right skills in fields like AI management, robotics maintenance, and customer experience design. The future of service jobs lies in collaboration between humans and machines, where technology takes on the mundane, and humans focus on what makes the service experience unique—personalization, creativity, and emotional intelligence.

This chapter explores the significant effects of automation in customer service, hospitality, and transportation. Let me know if you'd like further elaboration on any point or additional examples!

CHAPTER 11

THE GIG ECONOMY AND ROBOTICS

Introduction: The Convergence of the Gig Economy and Robotics

The rise of the **gig economy**—a labor market characterized by short-term contracts, freelance work, and flexible job opportunities—has transformed the way people work, offering freedom and autonomy while also creating instability and insecurity. As automation and robotics continue to develop, they are having a profound impact on the gig economy, creating both opportunities and challenges for workers. In this chapter, we will explore how robotics and automation intersect with the gig economy, shaping the future of work and altering the roles of gig workers across various sectors.

The Growth of the Gig Economy: A New Way of Working

The gig economy has grown rapidly over the past decade, largely driven by digital platforms that connect workers with customers. Companies like **Uber**, **Airbnb**, **TaskRabbit**, and **Freelancer.com** have enabled individuals to take on short-term jobs or freelance assignments, often with no long-term commitment or employment benefits. The flexibility of gig work appeals to many, offering the ability to choose when, where, and how much to work.

However, the gig economy is also associated with job insecurity, a lack of benefits like health insurance or retirement savings, and unpredictable income. Workers are considered independent contractors, which means they are responsible for their own expenses and lack the protections typically afforded to full-time employees, such as job security and worker's compensation.

The Role of Automation and Robotics in the Gig Economy

As automation and robotics become more integrated into the workforce, their impact on the gig economy is becoming increasingly apparent. On one hand, automation can create new gig opportunities, offering individuals the chance to work in emerging fields. On the other hand, it can replace certain types of gig work altogether, leading to job displacement and creating new challenges for workers.

For instance, in transportation, the rise of **autonomous vehicles** may significantly reduce the need for gig drivers. Similarly, in delivery services, autonomous drones or robots may take over the last-mile delivery process, reducing the demand for human couriers. As automation continues to penetrate various industries, gig workers must adapt to the evolving landscape or risk being displaced by robots.

The Impact of Robotics on Gig Work: Opportunities and Challenges

1. Automation in Delivery and Logistics

One of the most significant ways robotics and automation are intersecting with the gig economy is in the **delivery sector**. Traditional delivery jobs, such as food delivery or courier services, have been an integral part of the gig economy. However, with the rise of **autonomous delivery vehicles**, **drones**, and **robotic couriers**, many of these tasks are being taken over by machines.

Companies like **Amazon** and **Domino's Pizza** are already experimenting with autonomous delivery vehicles and drones. For example, Amazon has developed **Prime Air**, a drone-based delivery system, designed to deliver packages within 30 minutes. Similarly, **Starship Technologies** operates a fleet of small autonomous robots that deliver food and groceries to customers.

While these technological advancements are improving efficiency and reducing costs for companies, they may displace human delivery workers, especially in tasks that are repetitive and physically demanding. For gig workers, this means adapting to a new set of opportunities, such as operating or maintaining these robots, or finding new types of work that robots cannot yet do.

2. Gig Work in the Robotic Maintenance Sector

While automation may reduce the demand for some types of gig work, it is also creating entirely new fields and opportunities. As robotics and automation technologies proliferate, there is an increasing need for skilled workers who can manage, repair, and maintain these machines.

For instance, robots and AI-powered systems need regular servicing, software updates, and troubleshooting. Gig workers with expertise in **robotics maintenance**, **AI**

programming, and **robotics repair** will be in high demand. These jobs require specialized skills but offer the flexibility and autonomy associated with gig work.

Additionally, gig workers can be employed to oversee the operations of autonomous systems. In delivery services, for example, workers might be required to supervise drones or autonomous vehicles, ensuring they follow the correct routes, manage system errors, and ensure safety during deliveries. These new roles can provide gig workers with an opportunity to transition into high-tech, growing industries.

3. Automating the Gig Economy Platforms

Automation also has the potential to improve the gig economy itself by streamlining the platforms that connect gig workers with clients. **AI-powered platforms** can help match workers with tasks more efficiently by analyzing both the skills of the worker and the specific needs of the job. For example, a platform like **Uber** could use AI to not only match drivers with passengers but also optimize routes, reduce wait times, and increase earnings potential for drivers.

Additionally, AI can automate many aspects of gig work administration, such as payroll, scheduling, and dispute resolution. This can simplify the gig economy for workers, allowing them to focus more on their tasks and less on administrative tasks.

4. The Shift to Digital and Remote Gig Work

While traditional gig work often involves physical labor— such as driving, cleaning, or delivering goods—automation is enabling a shift toward **remote and digital gig work**. Many service-based gig jobs, such as customer service, virtual assistance, content creation, and freelance writing, can now be performed remotely, often with the help of automation.

AI-powered virtual assistants, like those used in customer service or tech support, can handle repetitive tasks, while human gig workers focus on more complex or nuanced customer interactions. Similarly, automation tools can assist with scheduling, communications, or marketing, allowing remote gig workers to manage multiple tasks more efficiently.

This shift toward digital work opens up new opportunities for people to engage in the gig economy regardless of geographic location. It also provides greater flexibility and access to gig opportunities for people with disabilities or other barriers to traditional, in-person work.

Challenges for Gig Workers in an Automated Economy

While there are many new opportunities created by automation, gig workers also face challenges as robots and AI begin to take over certain tasks. These challenges include:

1. **Job Displacement**: The rise of autonomous vehicles, drones, and robots may result in the displacement of gig workers who rely on physical labor, such as delivery drivers or warehouse workers. Gig workers in these sectors will need to upskill and transition to roles in maintenance, oversight, or technology.

2. **Increased Competition**: As automation improves efficiency, there will likely be an increase in competition among gig workers. For example, as platforms use AI to better match workers with tasks, workers may find it more challenging to secure high-paying gigs, especially if automation results in a glut of available labor.

3. **Job Insecurity**: The gig economy is already characterized by a lack of job security and benefits. As automation continues to change the landscape, gig workers may face even more uncertainty about their roles, as robots and AI systems may take over routine tasks or perform them more efficiently.

4. **Skill Gaps**: As automation creates new types of gig work, workers will need to upskill in areas like robotics maintenance, data analysis, AI programming, and machine learning. Workers who are unable or unwilling to learn these new skills may find themselves left behind in the increasingly automated workforce.

Conclusion: A New Era for Gig Workers in an Automated World

The gig economy is changing rapidly as automation and robotics reshape how work is performed. While automation presents exciting opportunities for gig workers, including new roles in robotics maintenance, digital work, and AI management, it also introduces significant challenges, such as job displacement, skill gaps, and increased competition. The future of gig work will require workers to adapt by acquiring new skills, embracing emerging technologies, and finding ways to thrive in a world where automation plays an ever-increasing role.

As automation continues to evolve, the gig economy will become more integrated with high-tech solutions, offering greater flexibility and new avenues for employment. However, ensuring that gig workers have the support and training they need to succeed in this rapidly changing landscape will be crucial for fostering a fair and sustainable future for all.

This chapter highlights how automation and robotics are shaping the gig economy, creating new opportunities and challenges for workers. Let me know if you'd like further expansion on any section or additional examples!

CHAPTER 12

JOB DISPLACEMENT AND THE FUTURE OF EMPLOYMENT

Introduction: The Dual Impact of Automation on Employment

Automation is rapidly changing the global job market, ushering in both opportunities and challenges. On one hand, robots, AI, and automated systems are increasing productivity, reducing costs, and creating new jobs in emerging fields. On the other hand, automation has the potential to displace workers, particularly in industries that rely on routine and manual tasks. This chapter takes a balanced look at how automation is likely to impact employment, examining the jobs that may be lost, the new opportunities that could arise, and the strategies that workers, businesses, and governments can adopt to ensure a smooth transition to a more automated workforce.

The Potential for Job Displacement

As automation technologies become more advanced, certain jobs—particularly those involving repetitive, manual, or low-skill tasks—are increasingly at risk of being automated. The most susceptible sectors to job displacement include:

1. **Manufacturing**: Historically, manufacturing has been one of the first sectors to embrace automation, starting with the introduction of assembly lines. Today, robots are capable of performing a wide range of tasks, from welding and assembly to quality control and packaging. While this improves efficiency and safety, it also reduces the need for human workers in these roles. As robotic systems and AI-driven automation continue to evolve, jobs in manufacturing will continue to decline.

2. **Transportation and Logistics**: The development of **autonomous vehicles**, including self-driving trucks, taxis, and drones, has the potential to displace millions of jobs in transportation. Long-haul truck drivers, delivery drivers, and taxi drivers are among the most vulnerable to automation. According to some estimates, over 3 million people in the U.S. alone work as truck drivers, a profession that could be significantly reduced with the widespread adoption of autonomous vehicles.

104

3. **Customer Service**: The rise of **AI-powered chatbots** and virtual assistants has already led to job displacement in customer service roles. Automated systems can handle routine inquiries, process transactions, and provide support 24/7, reducing the need for human customer service representatives. While complex or sensitive issues may still require human interaction, many low-skill customer service jobs may be replaced by automation in the future.

4. **Retail**: Retail jobs are increasingly threatened by automation, from **self-checkout machines** and cashierless stores to AI-driven recommendation engines. The rise of e-commerce and automated fulfillment centers is already transforming the retail landscape, and many traditional retail roles, such as cashiers, stock clerks, and floor attendants, are at risk of being replaced by automation.

5. **Agriculture**: In agriculture, **autonomous tractors**, robotic harvesters, and drones are taking over tasks that once required human labor. As automation continues to infiltrate farming operations, jobs like crop picking, weeding, and soil monitoring are likely to be automated, reducing the need for manual farmworkers.

How Automation Creates New Job Opportunities

While automation has the potential to displace certain jobs, it also creates new opportunities in sectors that require more advanced skills or are directly related to the development, maintenance, and management of automated systems. Some of the key areas where new jobs are likely to emerge include:

1. **Robotics and Automation Engineering**: As more businesses implement automation systems, there will be an increasing demand for engineers, technicians, and specialists in robotics and automation. Workers in these fields will be responsible for designing, building, and maintaining robotic systems, as well as developing software and AI algorithms that power these technologies. Automation engineering and AI programming will become essential skills in the future workforce.

2. **Data Science and AI**: The growing reliance on AI in industries such as healthcare, finance, retail, and logistics will drive the demand for workers with expertise in data science, machine learning, and AI development. Data scientists, machine learning engineers, and AI researchers will be needed to

create algorithms that can analyze vast amounts of data, make decisions, and optimize processes.

3. **Cybersecurity**: As more businesses and industries embrace automation, the need for robust cybersecurity measures becomes even more critical. With the increasing number of interconnected devices and AI systems, the demand for cybersecurity professionals will grow. These professionals will be responsible for protecting automated systems from cyberattacks, ensuring that sensitive data is secure and preventing disruptions in critical services.

4. **Healthcare**: While automation may displace certain jobs in healthcare, it will also create new opportunities in fields such as robotic surgery, telemedicine, and healthcare IT. Healthcare professionals will need to work alongside robots and AI-powered systems to provide better patient care, making roles in robotics-assisted surgery, medical device maintenance, and telehealth consultations increasingly important.

5. **Green and Sustainable Technologies**: Automation can also help advance efforts in sustainability, creating job opportunities in **green technologies** and

sustainable industries. For example, automated systems are being used to improve energy efficiency in buildings, optimize recycling processes, and manage renewable energy grids. New jobs will be created in sectors focused on reducing environmental impact and mitigating climate change.

6. **Personalized Services**: As robots take over repetitive tasks, human workers can focus on areas that require emotional intelligence, creativity, and problem-solving skills. This shift will create more opportunities for workers in customer-facing roles that require high levels of personalization, such as concierge services, personal shopping, and creative industries.

Skills for the Future: Preparing the Workforce for Automation

As automation changes the nature of work, it is essential that workers develop the skills needed to thrive in an automated economy. The future of employment will require a blend of **technical skills, problem-solving abilities**, and **soft skills**. Some of the key areas where workers will need to upskill include:

1. **STEM Education**: As the demand for robotics, AI, and data science grows, there will be an increasing need for workers with strong skills in science, technology, engineering, and mathematics (STEM). Fostering education and training in these fields will be essential for ensuring that workers are prepared for the jobs of the future.

2. **Adaptability and Lifelong Learning**: The rapid pace of technological change means that workers will need to continuously adapt and learn new skills. Lifelong learning, including reskilling and upskilling, will become a critical component of workforce development. Online courses, vocational training programs, and certifications will play a key role in helping workers transition to new careers.

3. **Human-Centered Skills**: While automation may replace many manual tasks, there will always be a demand for skills that require human judgment, creativity, and emotional intelligence. Roles in customer service, leadership, and creativity will still require a human touch, as automation cannot replicate the nuances of human interaction.

4. **Collaboration with Technology**: Rather than being displaced by robots, many workers will need to learn

how to collaborate with automated systems. For example, workers in fields like manufacturing, healthcare, and logistics will need to develop the skills to operate, troubleshoot, and manage robotic systems, ensuring that they work efficiently and safely alongside humans.

The Role of Governments and Businesses in Managing Job Displacement

Governments and businesses have a crucial role to play in managing the impact of automation on employment. Policy solutions and business strategies will be necessary to support workers as they transition into new roles and industries. Some potential solutions include:

1. **Universal Basic Income (UBI)**: Some economists and policymakers suggest that a Universal Basic Income—an unconditional cash payment to all citizens—could help offset job displacement caused by automation. UBI could provide a safety net for individuals who are unable to find new employment or who are transitioning to new industries.

2. **Retraining Programs**: Governments and businesses can partner to offer retraining programs that help

workers develop new skills in growing industries. These programs could focus on areas like technology, healthcare, and green energy, where job opportunities are expanding.

3. **Job Creation in New Sectors**: Governments can incentivize the creation of new jobs in sectors that are likely to grow in an automated economy, such as renewable energy, sustainable infrastructure, and AI development.

Conclusion: The Future of Employment in an Automated World

Automation will undoubtedly disrupt the job market, displacing certain jobs while also creating new opportunities in emerging fields. By embracing change, investing in education and training, and adopting policies that support workers, we can ensure that automation benefits everyone. The future of work will be shaped by the collaboration between humans and machines, where technology enhances human capabilities and creates a more efficient, sustainable, and innovative workforce.

This chapter provides a balanced view of the potential for job displacement and the new opportunities that automation can create, while also offering strategies for preparing the workforce for these changes. Let me know if you'd like further elaboration or specific examples added!

CHAPTER 13

THE SKILLS OF THE FUTURE: WHAT WORKERS WILL NEED

Introduction: Adapting to an Automated World

As automation and robotics continue to transform industries, the nature of work is evolving at an unprecedented pace. To remain relevant in an increasingly automated world, workers must adapt by acquiring new skills that complement, enhance, and coexist with emerging technologies. While certain traditional roles may disappear, new opportunities will emerge in fields that require a blend of technical expertise, creativity, emotional intelligence, and problem-solving abilities.

In this chapter, we will explore the key skill sets that workers will need to thrive in a world shaped by automation, highlighting the importance of both **technical skills** and **human-centered abilities**.

Technical Skills: Embracing Technology and Innovation

1. **Robotics and Automation Expertise**

As robots and automation become increasingly integrated into various industries, there will be a growing demand for workers with expertise in **robotics** and **automation technologies**. Workers will need to understand how robots are designed, programmed, and maintained. Skills in programming and operating robotic systems will be crucial, especially for roles in manufacturing, logistics, and healthcare.

- **Key Skills**: Robotics design, automation programming, robotics maintenance, sensor integration, and robotic systems management.
- **Career Opportunities**: Robotics engineers, automation technicians, systems integrators, and robotics maintenance specialists.

2. **Data Science and AI**

Artificial intelligence (AI) and machine learning (ML) are at the heart of automation, enabling machines to learn from data, adapt, and make decisions. Workers with expertise in data science and AI will be highly sought after. These professionals will analyze vast amounts of data, develop algorithms, and create AI systems that improve business processes, drive efficiency, and solve complex problems.

- **Key Skills**: Data analysis, machine learning, predictive modeling, AI programming, and data visualization.
- **Career Opportunities**: Data scientists, machine learning engineers, AI developers, and data analysts.

3. **Cybersecurity**

As industries become more reliant on automated systems and interconnected devices, the need for robust cybersecurity will grow exponentially. Cybersecurity professionals will play a critical role in protecting sensitive data, safeguarding automated systems from cyberattacks, and ensuring the integrity of the digital infrastructure that powers automation.

- **Key Skills**: Network security, encryption, ethical hacking, threat analysis, and risk management.
- **Career Opportunities**: Cybersecurity analysts, penetration testers, network security engineers, and data protection officers.

4. **Cloud Computing and Infrastructure Management**

Cloud computing provides the backbone for many automated systems, enabling businesses to scale operations and store vast amounts of data. As more companies embrace cloud-based automation solutions, workers with expertise in cloud computing and infrastructure management will be in high demand. These professionals will ensure that systems are running smoothly, efficiently, and securely.

- **Key Skills**: Cloud architecture, server management, virtualization, DevOps, and cloud security.
- **Career Opportunities**: Cloud engineers, cloud architects, IT infrastructure specialists, and systems administrators.

5. **Software Development and Programming**

While automation will replace some manual jobs, the need for skilled software developers and programmers will only grow. These professionals will create and maintain the software that powers automation, develop custom applications, and ensure the seamless integration of new technologies.

- **Key Skills**: Programming languages (e.g., Python, Java, C++), software development frameworks, application development, and system integration.

116

- **Career Opportunities**: Software engineers, application developers, systems programmers, and UI/UX designers.

Human-Centered Skills: What Machines Can't Do

While automation can handle repetitive and predictable tasks, there are many abilities that humans possess which machines cannot replicate. The ability to empathize, innovate, and think critically are human qualities that will remain in high demand.

1. **Creativity and Innovation**

As automation handles more routine tasks, human workers will be required to engage in **creative problem-solving** and **innovation**. In industries like marketing, design, and entertainment, creativity will be a key differentiator. Professionals who can use technology to generate fresh ideas, develop new products, and create compelling experiences will be highly valuable.

- **Key Skills**: Design thinking, product development, ideation, and innovation management.

117

- **Career Opportunities**: Product designers, creative directors, innovation consultants, and digital content creators.

2. **Emotional Intelligence and Interpersonal Skills**

Emotional intelligence (EQ), or the ability to understand and manage emotions, will be essential in roles that require interaction with others. Jobs in customer service, healthcare, education, and leadership will require workers to use their EQ to navigate complex social dynamics, provide emotional support, and manage teams effectively. These roles cannot be easily automated because they require empathy, understanding, and the ability to relate to others on a human level.

- **Key Skills**: Active listening, empathy, conflict resolution, leadership, and team collaboration.
- **Career Opportunities**: Customer service representatives, healthcare professionals, educators, HR managers, and team leaders.

3. **Critical Thinking and Problem-Solving**

The ability to analyze complex situations, identify problems, and develop creative solutions will remain one of the most sought-after skills in the workforce. While automation can provide data and insights, it is human judgment and reasoning that are needed to make the final decisions. In an automated world, workers who can critically assess situations and find innovative solutions will be indispensable.

- **Key Skills**: Analytical thinking, strategic planning, decision-making, and complex problem-solving.
- **Career Opportunities**: Managers, consultants, business analysts, and operations managers.

4. **Adaptability and Lifelong Learning**

The pace of technological change means that workers will need to be adaptable and committed to **lifelong learning**. As industries and technologies evolve, workers must continuously update their skills and stay informed about new developments in their fields. This will require a growth mindset and a willingness to embrace change.

- **Key Skills**: Self-directed learning, adaptability, resilience, and agility in the workplace.

- **Career Opportunities**: Professionals in all sectors, as lifelong learning will be essential for all types of jobs.

5. **Collaboration with Technology**

Rather than being replaced by machines, workers will increasingly need to collaborate with AI, robots, and automated systems. This requires a deep understanding of how these technologies work and the ability to integrate them into workflows effectively. The future workforce will need to be tech-savvy, comfortable working alongside automated systems, and able to leverage technology to augment their capabilities.

- **Key Skills**: Human-machine collaboration, tech literacy, digital communication, and system integration.
- **Career Opportunities**: Operations managers, robotics technicians, AI trainers, and systems analysts.

Conclusion: Preparing for the Future of Work

The future of work will be defined by a balance of **technical expertise** and **human-centered skills**. As automation continues to reshape industries, workers will need to embrace new technologies, upskill in emerging fields, and develop their ability to collaborate with machines. While automation will undoubtedly displace certain jobs, it will also create new opportunities for workers who are prepared to adapt and grow.

By focusing on a combination of hard and soft skills, workers can ensure their continued relevance in the workforce and thrive in an increasingly automated world. Governments, educational institutions, and businesses must play a key role in providing the training and support necessary to prepare workers for this rapidly changing landscape.

This chapter explores the skills workers will need to succeed in an increasingly automated world. Let me know if you'd like to expand on any section or explore specific skills in more detail!

CHAPTER 14

RETRAINING AND RESKILLING THE WORKFORCE

Introduction: The Need for Retraining and Reskilling in an Automated World

As automation continues to reshape industries, the demand for new skills is growing rapidly. While automation offers tremendous potential for increasing efficiency and productivity, it also displaces certain jobs, particularly those that involve routine, manual, and repetitive tasks. To address this challenge, workers must adapt by learning new skills, and education and training programs are evolving to meet this demand. Retraining and reskilling are crucial strategies for preparing the workforce for the jobs of the future. In this chapter, we will explore how education systems and corporate training programs are evolving to equip workers with the skills needed to thrive in a rapidly changing job market.

The Importance of Retraining and Reskilling

The impact of automation on the workforce is undeniable. Jobs in manufacturing, retail, transportation, and customer service are being affected by technological advancements that make certain tasks obsolete. As a result, workers must transition to new roles or industries that are less likely to be automated. This requires a shift in mindset and a commitment to learning new skills that are aligned with the needs of an increasingly digital economy.

Retraining and reskilling offer workers the opportunity to stay competitive in the job market, reduce the risk of unemployment, and take advantage of emerging job opportunities. In addition to benefiting individual workers, a well-trained and adaptable workforce is essential for ensuring that businesses remain innovative, productive, and resilient in the face of technological disruption.

The Evolution of Education and Training Programs

1. Digital Literacy and Tech-Driven Education

One of the most significant shifts in education and training is the emphasis on **digital literacy**. In today's world, having a basic understanding of how digital technologies work is no longer optional—it's a fundamental skill. As industries increasingly rely on digital tools, workers need to be proficient in using technology to perform tasks efficiently. This includes understanding how to use software, manage digital systems, and troubleshoot common issues.

In response to this need, educational institutions and training programs are incorporating digital literacy into their curricula. Schools, universities, and vocational programs are offering courses in coding, data management, cloud computing, and other tech-related fields to ensure that students and workers are prepared for the future of work.

For example, **coding bootcamps** like **Codecademy** and **Le Wagon** provide intensive, short-term training programs designed to teach people how to code and work with digital technologies. These programs offer an accessible and flexible way for individuals to learn new skills without committing to lengthy degree programs.

2. **Focus on STEM Education**

The growing demand for skilled workers in **science, technology, engineering, and mathematics (STEM)** fields is another driving force behind changes in education and training programs. STEM fields are closely aligned with the development of automation, AI, robotics, and data analytics, all of which are shaping the future of work. As automation continues to disrupt industries, there is an increasing need for workers with expertise in these areas to develop, maintain, and optimize the technologies that are driving change.

Many educational systems are placing a stronger emphasis on STEM education, from elementary school through to higher education. Governments and organizations are investing in initiatives aimed at increasing STEM engagement among students, especially in underrepresented groups, such as women and minorities. These efforts include after-school programs, mentorship opportunities, and scholarships designed to foster interest in STEM careers and ensure a diverse talent pool for the future workforce.

Additionally, many universities and technical colleges are offering **certifications** and **degree programs** focused on emerging technologies like artificial intelligence, machine learning, cybersecurity, and blockchain. These advanced programs provide specialized skills that are in high demand by employers in tech-driven industries.

3. **Corporate Training and Internal Reskilling Programs**

While traditional education systems are evolving to meet the needs of the future workforce, many workers will need to update their skills throughout their careers. As the pace of technological change accelerates, **corporate training** programs are becoming more critical. Employers recognize that investing in the development of their workforce is key to maintaining a competitive edge and ensuring business success in an automated world.

Corporate reskilling and upskilling programs help employees transition to new roles, learn new technologies, and acquire the skills necessary for the jobs of the future. **On-the-job training**, **mentorship**, and **online learning platforms** are increasingly common ways to provide ongoing education. For example, companies like **Google** and **Amazon** offer **reskilling programs** for employees, enabling them to gain new technical skills, such as cloud computing or machine learning, that align with the company's evolving needs.

Organizations are also turning to **online learning platforms** like **LinkedIn Learning**, **Coursera**, and **Udemy**, which offer a wide range of courses on topics ranging from digital marketing and project management to coding and AI. These platforms allow workers to learn at their own pace and on their own schedule, making it easier for employees to stay current with the latest trends in their field.

4. Microcredentials and Industry Certifications

In addition to traditional degrees, **microcredentials** and **industry certifications** are becoming increasingly popular in the workforce. These programs offer workers a way to gain specific, industry-recognized qualifications in a relatively short amount of time. For example, certifications in cloud computing, data science, and cybersecurity are highly regarded by employers and can significantly boost a worker's job prospects.

Microcredentials are particularly valuable in fields like IT and digital marketing, where skills and tools change rapidly. By obtaining certifications from reputable organizations, workers can demonstrate their expertise in emerging technologies and stay competitive in the job market.

Collaborative Efforts: Governments, Businesses, and Educational Institutions

1. Public-Private Partnerships

Governments, businesses, and educational institutions have a critical role to play in preparing the workforce for the future. Public-private partnerships are essential for creating a cohesive strategy for workforce development. For example, many countries are investing in **vocational training** programs and **apprenticeships** to provide workers with hands-on experience and practical skills in high-demand industries.

In addition, governments are implementing policies that incentivize companies to invest in reskilling programs. **Tax breaks**, **training subsidies**, and **grant programs** can encourage businesses to provide their workers with the tools they need to succeed in an automated world.

2. Universal Access to Education

One of the challenges in preparing workers for the future is ensuring that training and education opportunities are accessible to all. As automation affects industries around the world, it is crucial that no worker is left behind. Governments, employers, and educational institutions must work together to ensure that reskilling programs are

affordable, **inclusive**, and **widely available**, particularly for workers in vulnerable sectors, such as manufacturing or retail.

Many organizations are addressing this by providing **financial aid, scholarships**, and **low-cost training options** to make education more accessible. Additionally, online learning platforms have democratized education, allowing individuals from all backgrounds to access training and gain new skills from anywhere in the world.

The Role of Lifelong Learning

The rapid pace of technological change means that workers will need to commit to **lifelong learning** throughout their careers. Retraining and reskilling are not one-time events but rather ongoing processes that will evolve as new technologies and job markets emerge. The concept of lifelong learning is critical for fostering a workforce that can continuously adapt to changes in the economy and the nature of work.

Governments, businesses, and individuals must all prioritize the importance of continual learning, recognizing that the ability to **adapt and upskill** is essential for success in an increasingly automated world.

Conclusion: Preparing for the Future Through Retraining and Reskilling

Retraining and reskilling are essential strategies for preparing workers for the jobs of the future. As automation reshapes industries, it is crucial that workers have access to education and training programs that equip them with the skills needed to thrive in an increasingly digital economy. By focusing on both **technical expertise** and **human-centered skills**, workers can transition to new roles, embrace emerging technologies, and remain competitive in the future job market. Governments, businesses, and educational institutions must collaborate to ensure that the workforce is prepared for the challenges and opportunities presented by automation, paving the way for a more inclusive, resilient, and innovative workforce.

This chapter highlights the importance of retraining and reskilling to equip workers with the skills they need for the future. Let me know if you need more details on any specific aspect or additional examples!

CHAPTER 15

COLLABORATIVE ROBOTS: HUMANS AND MACHINES WORKING TOGETHER

Introduction: The Rise of Collaborative Robots (Cobots)

As automation continues to evolve, one of the most exciting advancements in robotics is the development of **collaborative robots**, or **cobots**. Unlike traditional industrial robots that often operate in isolation or behind safety barriers, cobots are designed to work alongside humans in a shared workspace. The integration of cobots into various industries is transforming the way tasks are performed, improving efficiency, safety, and productivity without displacing human workers. This chapter explores the role of cobots, how they are reshaping industries, and how they are enabling humans and machines to work together in harmony.

What Are Collaborative Robots (Cobots)?

Collaborative robots, or cobots, are robotic systems specifically designed to work alongside humans in a shared environment. Unlike traditional robots, which are often confined to specific areas or require safety fencing to prevent accidents, cobots are equipped with advanced sensors, AI, and machine learning algorithms that allow them to interact safely and effectively with human workers.

Cobots are typically lightweight, flexible, and easy to program, making them accessible to a wide range of industries. They can perform a variety of tasks, from repetitive assembly and material handling to complex operations requiring precision and dexterity. Cobots are designed to enhance human capabilities rather than replace them, allowing workers to focus on higher-level tasks while leaving the repetitive or physically demanding work to the robots.

The Role of Cobots in Various Industries

Cobots are increasingly being deployed across a wide range of industries, from manufacturing and logistics to healthcare and agriculture. Here are some key sectors where cobots are making a significant impact:

1. Manufacturing: Enhancing Efficiency and Safety

The manufacturing industry has been one of the earliest adopters of cobots. In this environment, cobots work alongside human operators to perform tasks such as assembly, welding, painting, and quality control. These robots are particularly useful in handling tasks that are repetitive, physically demanding, or dangerous, allowing human workers to focus on more complex or creative aspects of production.

For example, **Universal Robots**, a leading provider of cobots, has developed robots that can be easily programmed to handle assembly tasks, like screwing or placing components, at a fraction of the time it would take for a human to perform the same job. These cobots improve efficiency by working tirelessly and with high precision, reducing errors and waste, while also improving workplace safety by taking over hazardous tasks like lifting heavy objects or working in dangerous environments.

Key Benefits for Manufacturing:

- Increased productivity by automating repetitive tasks.

- Improved safety by reducing worker exposure to dangerous tasks.
- Greater flexibility, as cobots can easily be reprogrammed for different tasks or products.
- Lower costs due to reduced errors and greater operational efficiency.

2. **Logistics and Warehousing: Optimizing Order Fulfillment**

In logistics and warehousing, cobots are transforming the way goods are stored, picked, and shipped. These robots are capable of navigating warehouses, picking up items, and delivering them to human workers for further processing. Cobots work in tandem with warehouse employees, improving the speed and accuracy of order fulfillment without the need for extensive reorganization of workflows.

For example, **Amazon Robotics**, a subsidiary of Amazon, uses mobile cobots in its fulfillment centers to transport items between different areas of the warehouse. These robots autonomously move products from storage shelves to human workers, who then complete the packaging and shipping process. This integration of cobots helps Amazon fulfill orders faster and more efficiently while reducing the physical strain on warehouse employees.

Key Benefits for Logistics:

- Increased order fulfillment speed and accuracy.
- Reduced labor costs by automating material handling tasks.
- Improved worker safety by minimizing physical strain and exposure to hazardous environments.
- Enhanced scalability, as cobots can handle peak demands without the need for additional workforce.

3. Healthcare: Assisting in Surgery and Patient Care

Cobots are making strides in the healthcare sector, where their ability to enhance precision and assist in complex procedures is proving invaluable. In **robotic surgery**, cobots work alongside surgeons, providing enhanced accuracy and control during operations. These systems are designed to make surgical procedures less invasive, reduce recovery times, and improve patient outcomes.

One notable example is the **da Vinci Surgical System**, a robotic platform that enables surgeons to perform minimally invasive surgeries with high precision. The system's robotic arms are guided by the surgeon's hand movements, but the cobot provides additional dexterity and stability. Similarly, in patient care, cobots are being used to assist in rehabilitation, helping patients perform physical therapy exercises with the guidance of a robot that ensures proper technique and progress.

Key Benefits for Healthcare:

- Enhanced surgical precision, reducing the risk of complications.
- Improved patient recovery times due to minimally invasive procedures.
- Increased accessibility to healthcare by automating routine medical tasks.
- Better patient monitoring and rehabilitation assistance with robotic systems.

4. **Agriculture: Enhancing Precision and Productivity**

In agriculture, cobots are being used to optimize farming processes, from planting and irrigation to harvesting. These robots work alongside farmers to monitor crop health, detect pests, and even pick fruit. Cobots allow for more precise farming practices, improving crop yields and reducing waste while minimizing the need for manual labor.

For example, **Octinion's Rubion** is a robot designed to harvest strawberries autonomously. It uses machine vision to detect ripe fruit and picks it with care, reducing the likelihood of bruising and waste. This enables farmers to maintain high-quality crops while improving operational efficiency.

Key Benefits for Agriculture:

- Increased precision in planting, irrigation, and harvesting.
- Reduced labor costs by automating tasks that are repetitive or physically demanding.
- Improved sustainability by reducing pesticide use and optimizing resource allocation.
- Enhanced crop yields due to more effective monitoring and intervention.

The Human-Machine Partnership: How Cobots Complement Workers

Cobots are designed to collaborate with humans, rather than replace them, making them a valuable tool in various industries. The key difference between cobots and traditional robots is that cobots are meant to work alongside humans, enhancing their capabilities and improving productivity. Cobots do not eliminate the need for human workers; instead, they free up workers from tedious or dangerous tasks and enable them to focus on more strategic, creative, or complex work.

For example, in manufacturing, a human worker may oversee the cobot while focusing on tasks that require judgment or decision-making, such as managing inventory or inspecting quality. In healthcare, surgeons can rely on cobots to perform repetitive or precise movements while making critical decisions during surgery. By acting as a helper, cobots allow workers to focus on tasks that require human intelligence, creativity, and emotional engagement.

Key Benefits for Workers:

- Reduced physical strain and risk of injury by taking over repetitive or dangerous tasks.

139

- Increased job satisfaction as workers are freed up to engage in more meaningful and intellectually stimulating tasks.
- Greater collaboration between human intelligence and robotic precision, leading to higher-quality outcomes.

The Future of Cobots: Expanding Their Role in the Workforce

As technology advances, the role of cobots is expected to expand significantly. Future cobots will become even more sophisticated, capable of performing a wider range of tasks with greater autonomy and precision. They will increasingly be integrated into industries that have traditionally been reliant on human labor, such as construction, food service, and education.

The ongoing development of **AI and machine learning** will enable cobots to adapt to new environments, learn from human workers, and make decisions in real time. As the cost of robotics technology continues to decrease, cobots will become more accessible to small and medium-sized businesses, further broadening their impact on industries around the world.

Conclusion: Humans and Machines, Working Together

Collaborative robots are transforming industries by enabling humans and machines to work together in more efficient and productive ways. By complementing human skills, cobots enhance precision, reduce physical strain, and increase safety without replacing workers. The future of work lies in the collaboration between human intelligence and robotic efficiency, where both can work in tandem to achieve optimal results. As automation continues to evolve, cobots will play an increasingly important role in shaping the workforce of tomorrow, providing workers with the tools they need to succeed in an automated world.

This chapter delves into the role of collaborative robots (cobots) and how they are reshaping industries. Let me know if you'd like more details on specific applications or further examples!

CHAPTER 16

THE ROLE OF ROBOTS IN DANGEROUS JOBS

Introduction: The Promise of Robots in High-Risk Jobs

Certain jobs have always been associated with high risks, requiring workers to face dangerous environments, hazardous materials, and life-threatening situations. In industries such as mining, firefighting, and disaster response, workers are often exposed to dangers that put their health and safety at risk. However, with the rise of robotics and automation, robots are increasingly being deployed to take over these high-risk jobs, improving safety for human workers and enhancing operational efficiency.

In this chapter, we will explore the growing role of robots in dangerous jobs, how they are being used in critical sectors, and the benefits they bring in terms of safety, efficiency, and operational effectiveness.

The Role of Robots in Mining: Reducing Hazards in the Deep

Mining is one of the most dangerous industries in the world, with workers regularly exposed to risks such as collapsing tunnels, toxic gases, and heavy machinery accidents. The introduction of robots into mining operations is helping reduce these hazards by taking over the most dangerous tasks and improving the overall safety of mining environments.

1. Autonomous Mining Vehicles and Equipment

One of the primary applications of robotics in mining is the use of **autonomous vehicles** and machinery to carry out tasks such as drilling, blasting, and transporting materials. Autonomous trucks and loaders, equipped with sensors and GPS technology, can navigate the mining site without human intervention, reducing the need for workers to operate heavy machinery in hazardous areas.

For example, **Rio Tinto**, a global mining company, has deployed autonomous trucks in its Australian mining operations. These trucks can haul materials from one part of the mine to another without the need for a driver, minimizing the risk of accidents. Similarly, **Caterpillar** and **Komatsu** offer autonomous mining equipment, such as drills and loaders, that can operate in dangerous conditions, ensuring that workers are kept at a safe distance from potential risks.

2. **Robotic Exploration and Inspection**

In addition to autonomous vehicles, robots are also being used to explore and inspect underground mines. Robotic systems equipped with cameras, sensors, and other monitoring equipment can be deployed to assess the stability of tunnels, detect gas leaks, and monitor environmental conditions. These robots can access areas that would be too dangerous for human workers, gathering critical data to prevent accidents and improve mine safety.

For example, **Minetec**, a company specializing in mining technology, has developed robotic inspection systems that can travel through tunnels to collect environmental data. This allows mining companies to monitor air quality, temperature, and humidity levels, providing real-time information about potential hazards.

The Role of Robots in Firefighting: Tackling Blazes from a Safe Distance

Firefighting is another high-risk profession, with firefighters often exposed to extreme heat, toxic smoke, and dangerous structures. Robots and drones are increasingly being used in firefighting operations to reduce the risk to human firefighters and enhance the effectiveness of emergency responses.

1. Firefighting Drones

Drones equipped with thermal imaging cameras and sensors are being used to assist firefighters by providing real-time aerial views of fire scenes. These drones can help firefighters assess the extent of the fire, identify hotspots, and determine the best approach for containing the blaze. Drones can also be used to deliver firefighting equipment or chemicals to areas that are too dangerous for humans to access.

For instance, **DJI**, a leading drone manufacturer, has developed firefighting drones that are capable of carrying payloads such as fire retardant or water to high-risk areas. These drones can operate in environments that are difficult for human firefighters to access, such as tall buildings or hazardous terrains, significantly improving response times and safety.

2. Robotic Firefighting Systems

In addition to drones, robots are being developed to fight fires directly. These **firefighting robots** are equipped with fire suppression systems, such as water hoses or foam dispensers, and can operate autonomously or under human control. These robots are designed to enter hazardous environments, such as burning buildings or chemical plants, and extinguish fires without putting human lives at risk.

For example, **Squirt**, a firefighting robot developed by **Industrial Firefighting**, is designed to navigate industrial environments to extinguish flames in places that are difficult to reach with traditional firefighting methods. It can be deployed in environments with intense heat and smoke, ensuring that human firefighters do not have to enter dangerous spaces.

The Role of Robots in Disaster Response: Saving Lives in Extreme Conditions

In disaster scenarios—whether due to natural events like earthquakes, floods, and hurricanes, or human-made incidents such as industrial accidents or terrorist attacks— human responders often face perilous conditions. Robots play a crucial role in disaster response by providing search- and-rescue operations, assessing structural damage, and delivering supplies in areas that are too dangerous for humans to enter.

1. Search-and-Rescue Robots

One of the most important applications of robots in disaster response is **search-and-rescue operations**. Robots equipped with cameras, sensors, and robotic arms can navigate collapsed buildings or other hazardous environments to search for survivors. These robots can access areas that are too dangerous for human rescuers, such as buildings that have been structurally compromised or contaminated zones.

For example, the **PackBot**, developed by **iRobot**, has been used in disaster response scenarios, including the 2011 Fukushima nuclear disaster. The PackBot is equipped with cameras and sensors that allow rescue teams to search for survivors and assess damage in dangerous environments. It can climb stairs, navigate rubble, and transmit real-time data to human operators, significantly enhancing rescue efforts.

2. Robotic Drones for Aerial Surveying

Drones are also playing an essential role in disaster response by providing real-time aerial surveys of affected areas.

147

Equipped with high-resolution cameras and infrared sensors, drones can quickly assess damage, locate victims, and guide rescue operations. These drones can cover large areas in a short amount of time, providing valuable information to emergency teams on the ground.

For instance, after natural disasters such as earthquakes or hurricanes, drones are used to assess infrastructure damage, locate blocked roads, and identify areas that need immediate attention. This helps emergency responders prioritize their efforts and allocate resources more effectively.

3. Delivery of Supplies and Medical Assistance

In addition to search-and-rescue operations, robots are also used to deliver critical supplies, such as food, water, and medical equipment, to disaster-stricken areas. **Robotic delivery systems** and drones can carry essential supplies to places that are difficult to access due to debris, flooding, or dangerous conditions.

For example, **Matternet**, a drone logistics company, has developed a system for delivering medical supplies to remote or disaster-affected areas. These drones are capable of carrying medical equipment, vaccines, and blood samples, ensuring that patients receive the care they need even in the most challenging environments.

The Benefits of Robots in Dangerous Jobs

1. Improved Safety for Workers

The primary benefit of using robots in dangerous jobs is the **reduction in human exposure to hazardous environments**. Robots can take on tasks that would otherwise put human lives at risk, such as handling hazardous materials, entering burning buildings, or working in unstable mine tunnels. This reduces the likelihood of injuries or fatalities, improving overall safety in high-risk industries.

2. Increased Efficiency and Speed

Robots can operate continuously without fatigue, allowing them to perform tasks at a much faster rate than human workers. In disaster response, for example, robots can search large areas or transport supplies quickly, helping to save lives and expedite rescue efforts. In firefighting and mining, robots can carry out tasks with high precision and consistency, improving efficiency and reducing delays.

3. Enhanced Precision and Accuracy

Robots are equipped with sensors, cameras, and AI systems that allow them to perform tasks with incredible precision. Whether it's identifying the exact location of a fire hotspot, assessing structural damage after an earthquake, or drilling in a mine with high accuracy, robots can complete tasks that require fine-tuned control, reducing human error and improving the quality of the work.

Conclusion: The Future of Robots in Dangerous Jobs

Robots are playing an increasingly important role in high-risk industries, helping to improve safety, efficiency, and effectiveness in jobs that involve significant hazards. As technology continues to evolve, robots will become even more capable of taking on dangerous tasks in mining, firefighting, disaster response, and beyond. The future of work in these industries will involve a combination of human expertise and robotic assistance, with robots enhancing human capabilities and protecting workers from life-threatening situations.

This chapter highlights the crucial role of robots in dangerous jobs, demonstrating how they improve safety and efficiency in high-risk sectors. Let me know if you'd like to expand on any section or explore other examples!

CHAPTER 17

AUTONOMOUS VEHICLES AND THE FUTURE OF TRANSPORTATION JOBS

Introduction: The Dawn of Autonomous Vehicles

Self-driving or **autonomous vehicles (AVs)** are quickly emerging as one of the most revolutionary technological advancements of the 21st century. From cars and trucks to drones and delivery robots, autonomous vehicles are poised to reshape the transportation and logistics industries. While these vehicles promise greater efficiency, reduced costs, and enhanced safety, they also bring significant changes to the workforce, particularly in sectors heavily reliant on human drivers and operators.

In this chapter, we will examine the impact of autonomous vehicles on transportation and logistics jobs, including the potential for job displacement, new opportunities, and the role that automation will play in the future of work in these industries.

The Rise of Autonomous Vehicles

Autonomous vehicles rely on a combination of **AI, machine learning, sensors, cameras,** and **GPS** technology to navigate their environment without human input. These vehicles can process vast amounts of data from their surroundings, allowing them to make decisions, avoid obstacles, and travel from one location to another autonomously.

The technology behind AVs has made significant strides in recent years, with major automakers and tech companies such as **Waymo** (a subsidiary of Alphabet), **Tesla, Uber,** and **Cruise** investing heavily in self-driving cars, trucks, and delivery drones. While fully autonomous vehicles are still in the testing phase in many regions, the widespread adoption of self-driving technology is expected to occur in the next few decades, with some areas already using semi-autonomous vehicles in limited applications.

The Impact on Transportation Jobs: Job Displacement Concerns

1. **Displacement of Truck Drivers**

One of the most significant impacts of autonomous vehicles will be on the trucking industry. In the United States alone, there are over 3 million truck drivers, many of whom work in long-haul transportation, delivering goods across the country. Autonomous trucks, which are capable of navigating highways without human input, pose a direct threat to these workers.

While fully autonomous trucks are not yet widely deployed, companies like **Tesla**, **Waymo**, and **TuSimple** are actively testing autonomous trucks with the goal of reducing the reliance on human drivers. These trucks promise to improve fuel efficiency, reduce delivery times, and lower labor costs. However, the potential loss of millions of truck driving jobs is a major concern, particularly for individuals who depend on this work for their livelihoods.

Despite the potential job displacement, it is important to note that the transition to autonomous trucks will likely happen gradually. While long-haul trucking may be automated in the future, many experts believe that short-haul trucking and last-mile delivery will continue to require human drivers for the foreseeable future.

2. Job Loss in Taxi and Ride-Hailing Services

Another sector heavily impacted by autonomous vehicles is **ride-hailing services** like **Uber** and **Lyft**. As self-driving cars become more advanced, the need for human drivers in these services may diminish. The rise of autonomous vehicles promises to reduce operational costs for ride-hailing companies by eliminating the need to pay human drivers, which could lead to significant job losses.

Autonomous taxis, also known as **robotaxis**, are already being tested in cities such as Phoenix and San Francisco. Companies like **Waymo** and **Cruise** have developed fleets of self-driving vehicles that transport passengers without human intervention. If these robotaxis gain widespread adoption, millions of taxi and ride-hailing drivers could lose their jobs.

3. Impact on Delivery and Logistics Jobs

Autonomous vehicles are also set to impact jobs in the **delivery** and **logistics** sectors. Companies like **Amazon** and **FedEx** are already experimenting with autonomous delivery vans, drones, and robots to transport packages more efficiently. Self-driving delivery vehicles have the potential to reduce the need for delivery drivers, particularly in areas where last-mile delivery is a key challenge.

For example, **Amazon Prime Air** is developing autonomous drones to deliver small packages directly to customers' doorsteps. Similarly, **Nuro**, a robotics company, has developed an autonomous vehicle designed for local deliveries. These technologies could significantly reduce labor costs in the logistics sector, but they also threaten jobs for delivery drivers, couriers, and warehouse staff.

The Emergence of New Opportunities: Jobs in the Autonomous Vehicle Ecosystem

While the rise of autonomous vehicles will lead to job displacement in certain areas, it will also create new opportunities for workers in industries that support the development, maintenance, and integration of these technologies. Here are some of the emerging job roles in the autonomous vehicle ecosystem:

1. **Autonomous Vehicle Technicians and Maintenance Specialists**

As autonomous vehicles become more widespread, the demand for skilled technicians who can maintain and repair these complex systems will increase. These technicians will be responsible for ensuring that the hardware and software systems in autonomous vehicles are functioning correctly, as well as performing regular maintenance and troubleshooting when issues arise.

Job roles in this field will require expertise in robotics, AI, machine learning, and sensor systems. Workers will need to be trained to understand the intricacies of autonomous vehicle systems, including their sensors, cameras, and communication networks.

2. AI and Robotics Engineers

The development of autonomous vehicles is driven by advances in AI and robotics. Engineers who specialize in machine learning, robotics, computer vision, and sensor integration will be in high demand to design, develop, and improve autonomous driving systems. These professionals will play a crucial role in ensuring that self-driving vehicles can navigate complex environments, interpret data accurately, and make real-time decisions.

3. Cybersecurity Specialists

As autonomous vehicles become more connected and rely on data sharing, the need for cybersecurity professionals will grow. These vehicles will be vulnerable to cyberattacks, which could compromise their safety and functionality. Cybersecurity experts will be needed to safeguard autonomous vehicles from hacking, ensure secure data transmission, and protect user privacy.

4. Autonomous Vehicle Data Analysts

Autonomous vehicles generate vast amounts of data from sensors, cameras, GPS systems, and other sources. Data analysts will be needed to analyze this data to improve the performance of autonomous vehicles, optimize routes, and ensure safety. These analysts will also use data to monitor vehicle performance, predict maintenance needs, and identify potential hazards.

5. New Roles in Last-Mile Delivery

While autonomous vehicles may replace some delivery drivers, they will also create new roles in last-mile delivery. Workers will be needed to manage autonomous delivery fleets, oversee the operation of delivery drones, and ensure the safe and timely delivery of goods. These new roles will require a mix of logistics management, robotics oversight, and customer service skills.

The Future of Transportation Jobs: Transitioning to New Roles

The shift toward autonomous vehicles will undoubtedly lead to significant changes in the transportation and logistics job market. However, the complete elimination of transportation jobs is unlikely to happen overnight. Instead, there will likely be a gradual transition as industries adopt autonomous technology at different rates and as human workers take on new roles that complement automation.

To support this transition, workers will need access to **reskilling** and **upskilling** programs that help them adapt to new job requirements. Governments, educational institutions, and companies should collaborate to provide training in emerging fields, such as AI, robotics, and autonomous vehicle maintenance, to ensure that workers are prepared for the evolving job market.

Conclusion: Embracing the Future of Transportation

Autonomous vehicles have the potential to revolutionize transportation and logistics, improving efficiency, reducing costs, and enhancing safety. However, this shift will also have profound effects on the workforce, particularly for drivers and delivery personnel. While some jobs will be displaced, the rise of autonomous vehicles will also create new opportunities in fields related to AI, robotics, cybersecurity, and logistics management.

By embracing the opportunities that automation presents and investing in training and reskilling, workers can adapt to the changing job market and thrive in the future of transportation. The future of work in this sector will be one of collaboration between humans and machines, where technology augments human capabilities and enables a safer, more efficient, and innovative transportation system.

This chapter explores how autonomous vehicles will impact jobs in transportation and logistics, discussing both the challenges and opportunities that arise from this shift. Let me know if you'd like more information on specific examples or further details!

CHAPTER 18

AUTOMATION IN THE CREATIVE INDUSTRIES

Introduction: The Intersection of Creativity and Automation

The creative industries—ranging from visual arts and music to fashion and advertising—have long been driven by human ingenuity, imagination, and emotion. However, as technology continues to evolve, automation and robotics are beginning to play a significant role in the creative process. From **AI-generated art** to **automated design systems**, these technologies are influencing creativity in ways that were once unimaginable, allowing for new forms of expression and innovation.

In this chapter, we will explore how automation and robotics are impacting the creative industries, from generating art and music to streamlining design workflows. We'll examine the ways these technologies are enhancing human creativity, raising new questions about the nature of art, and challenging traditional boundaries of creativity.

161

AI-Generated Art: The Rise of Machines as Creators

One of the most significant developments in the creative industries is the rise of **AI-generated art**. AI algorithms, particularly those based on **machine learning** and **deep learning**, can now create visual art that mimics the styles of famous artists or generates entirely new pieces. AI has the ability to analyze vast datasets of art, learning patterns, styles, and techniques to produce images, paintings, and sculptures that reflect its own interpretation of artistic expression.

1. Machine Learning in Art Creation

AI programs such as **DeepArt**, **DALL·E**, and **Artbreeder** are using machine learning algorithms to generate stunning visual works of art. By training neural networks on thousands of existing artworks, these systems can produce new, unique images based on prompts given by the user. For example, **DALL·E** uses GPT-3, an advanced language processing model, to generate images from textual descriptions, allowing users to create anything from "a cat riding a skateboard" to "a futuristic city in space."

While AI-generated art may seem like a novelty, its growing popularity has raised important questions about the nature of creativity and authorship. Can a machine truly be considered an artist? Do we attribute the creative process to the human who programmed the algorithm, or the algorithm itself?

2. AI as a Tool for Artists

While AI is capable of generating art, it's not just about replacing human creators. Many artists are now using AI as a **collaborative tool** to enhance their creative process. Artists can train AI models on their own works or integrate AI-generated elements into their designs, leading to hybrid forms of artwork that combine human intuition with machine precision.

For example, digital artist **Refik Anadol** uses AI to create immersive, data-driven art installations. He combines real-world data, such as weather patterns or urban activity, with machine learning algorithms to create abstract visualizations. This approach marries human creativity with the computational power of AI, pushing the boundaries of what's possible in the art world.

Automated Design Processes: Streamlining Creativity

Automation is also revolutionizing the design process across various creative industries, including graphic design, fashion, architecture, and advertising. By automating repetitive tasks, AI and robotics are enabling designers to focus on more high-level creative work, enhancing efficiency and opening up new possibilities for innovation.

1. **Automated Graphic Design and Branding**

In graphic design, tools like **Canva**, **Adobe Sensei**, and **Crello** are using AI to automate design elements, making it easier for both professionals and amateurs to create stunning visuals. These platforms can automatically adjust the layout, color scheme, and typography based on user inputs, such as brand guidelines or specific design trends.

For example, Adobe's **Sensei AI** can recognize objects and themes within an image, suggesting design adjustments and automatically resizing assets for different platforms. This saves designers significant time and effort, allowing them to focus more on creative ideation rather than manual adjustments.

While these tools can automate certain aspects of the design process, they also provide designers with new forms of creative input. By integrating AI suggestions, designers can explore different styles, layouts, and compositions more efficiently, leading to more dynamic and innovative designs.

2. Fashion Design and 3D Modeling

In fashion, AI and automation are streamlining the design process and allowing for **personalized clothing experiences**. Fashion houses and apparel brands are using AI to predict trends, design new collections, and optimize production. AI algorithms analyze consumer behavior, social media trends, and past purchasing patterns to predict which styles and fabrics will be popular in upcoming seasons.

Additionally, **3D modeling and digital fashion design** are becoming integral parts of the fashion industry. Designers are using AI-powered tools to create digital prototypes of garments, experimenting with textures, colors, and fit without needing to physically create samples. This reduces waste, speeds up the design process, and opens up new creative possibilities. Tools like **CLO 3D** and **Browzwear** enable fashion designers to visualize clothing in a virtual environment, making adjustments in real time before moving to production.

165

3. Architecture and Automated Building Design

In architecture, AI and automation are being used to design and visualize buildings more efficiently. **Generative design** algorithms, powered by AI, can create complex architectural structures by analyzing parameters such as material types, environmental factors, and building codes. These algorithms can generate multiple design options, offering architects a range of possibilities that may not have been considered during traditional design processes.

For example, **Autodesk's Revit** and **Fusion 360** use generative design to create optimized architectural plans and 3D models. These AI-powered tools analyze data and propose designs that maximize space, reduce material usage, and ensure energy efficiency. Generative design is pushing the boundaries of what's possible in architecture, allowing designers to create buildings that are not only aesthetically pleasing but also highly functional and sustainable.

Robots in Creative Production: Automation in Manufacturing and Art

While robots have traditionally been used in manufacturing to assemble products, they are now being integrated into

166

creative production as well. In the visual arts, robots are being used to create large-scale sculptures, paint murals, and even **print 3D artwork**.

1. **Robotic Art Creation**

Robots equipped with **artistic tools** can replicate the movements of human artists or even create entirely new art forms. For example, **The e-David Robot**, developed by researchers at the University of Konstanz, is a robot that can paint canvases with brushes, mimicking the techniques of human artists. It uses machine learning to analyze existing artwork and then generates its own pieces, offering a fascinating fusion of technology and traditional artistry.

In the realm of **3D printing**, robots are creating sculptures and installations that push the boundaries of physical art. These robots use a variety of materials, from clay to metal, to create intricate, three-dimensional pieces that would be difficult or impossible for human hands to produce. **KUKA Robotics** is a leading company that integrates robotic arms into art production, allowing for precise, automated creation of sculptural works.

The Role of Automation in Music and Sound Creation

In music, automation is not just about creating beats or compositions but also about generating new ways of composing and producing music. **AI music generators**, like **AIVA** and **Amper Music**, are creating entire compositions based on given inputs such as genre, mood, and instruments. These platforms use AI algorithms to analyze existing music and produce original compositions.

1. AI-Generated Music

AI-driven music platforms are democratizing music production by enabling anyone—regardless of their musical training—to create complex compositions. Musicians are using AI tools to experiment with different sounds, melodies, and rhythms, leading to innovative music production that pushes creative boundaries. While AI may generate the basic structure of a song, human musicians can further refine it, adding emotional depth and nuance that AI alone cannot replicate.

The Ethical Considerations of AI in Creativity

While AI and automation are providing new tools for creativity, they also raise ethical questions about authorship, copyright, and the role of machines in the creative process.

Who owns the rights to AI-generated art or music? Should AI be credited as a co-creator, or should the human who programmed the system take full credit? These are questions that will need to be addressed as AI continues to play a larger role in creative industries.

Additionally, as automation takes over some creative tasks, there is the potential for job displacement. Designers, artists, musicians, and other creative professionals may need to adapt to the changing landscape by learning how to work alongside AI tools and find new ways to integrate these technologies into their creative workflows.

Conclusion: Automation as a Catalyst for Creative Innovation

Automation and robotics are reshaping the creative industries in profound ways. AI-generated art, automated design processes, and robotic creative production are opening up new possibilities for innovation and expression. These technologies are not replacing human creativity but rather enhancing it, providing new tools that empower creators to push the boundaries of what's possible.

The future of the creative industries lies in collaboration between humans and machines, where automation complements human ingenuity and allows for new forms of art, music, design, and storytelling. As technology continues to evolve, it will be crucial for creative professionals to embrace these changes and harness the power of automation to fuel their work.

This chapter examines the impact of automation and robotics on creativity, from AI-generated art to automated design and robotic creativity. Let me know if you'd like to delve deeper into any specific applications or add more examples!

CHAPTER 19

ETHICS OF AUTOMATION AND ROBOTICS

Introduction: The Ethical Implications of Automation

The rapid advancement of automation and robotics has brought about profound changes to industries and societies around the world. While automation promises significant benefits, including increased efficiency, reduced costs, and improved safety, it also raises important ethical questions. These questions revolve around the impact of automation on human labor, fairness in the distribution of benefits, accountability for automated systems, and the broader societal implications of replacing human workers with machines.

As automation becomes increasingly integrated into the workforce and everyday life, it is crucial to address these ethical challenges to ensure that the technology is deployed in a manner that benefits everyone. In this chapter, we will explore the ethical dilemmas posed by automation, focusing on **job displacement**, **fairness**, and **accountability**, and consider how society can navigate these challenges.

Job Displacement: The Future of Work in an Automated World

One of the most pressing ethical concerns surrounding automation is its potential to displace millions of workers. The rise of autonomous vehicles, AI-powered robots, and automated systems in manufacturing, transportation, retail, and many other sectors threatens to replace human labor in roles that are repetitive, manual, or low-skilled. While automation can increase productivity and reduce costs for businesses, the displacement of workers poses significant challenges for individuals, families, and communities.

1. The Ethics of Job Displacement

Job displacement raises important ethical questions about **economic justice** and the **fairness** of a system that rewards technological innovation while leaving displaced workers without adequate support. The ethical dilemma centers on whether society should prioritize the benefits of automation—such as lower prices, increased efficiency, and reduced human error—or whether we should focus on protecting the livelihoods of workers who may be left behind by these technological advances.

For example, the rise of **autonomous trucks** in the transportation industry could displace millions of truck drivers, a job that has traditionally provided stable employment for individuals with limited education. Similarly, the automation of manufacturing processes could lead to job losses for factory workers. In these cases, the question becomes: How can we balance the economic gains from automation with the social costs of job displacement?

2. Reskilling and Retraining Workers

One potential solution to the ethical issue of job displacement is **reskilling** and **retraining** workers. By providing opportunities for workers to acquire new skills, society can help displaced workers transition to new roles in emerging fields, such as technology, healthcare, and green energy. While reskilling is a promising solution, it is not without challenges. Retraining workers requires significant investment in education and training programs, and not all displaced workers may have the resources or the ability to acquire new skills.

Ethically, it is important to ensure that reskilling programs are accessible to everyone, particularly workers in low-income or underserved communities. If automation leads to job displacement, but society invests in reskilling and education programs, workers may have a better chance at transitioning into new roles without experiencing economic hardship.

Fairness: Ensuring Equitable Access to the Benefits of Automation

Automation has the potential to create significant wealth and efficiency, but it also raises concerns about the **fair distribution of these benefits**. If the profits from automation are concentrated in the hands of a few individuals or corporations, it could exacerbate existing inequalities and widen the wealth gap between the rich and the poor. The ethical challenge here is to ensure that the benefits of automation are distributed fairly, and that the technology does not perpetuate or deepen economic disparities.

1. **Economic Inequality and Access to Technology**

In industries like **manufacturing, logistics,** and **agriculture**, automation is often associated with the creation of higher productivity and lower costs. However, the benefits of these efficiencies may not always be shared equally. Large corporations that adopt automation technologies may see significant profits, but workers in lower-skilled jobs may experience wage stagnation or job displacement.

To address these concerns, policymakers must consider strategies to **redistribute the economic gains** of automation. Some propose **universal basic income (UBI)** as a way to ensure that everyone has access to a basic standard of living, regardless of their employment status. UBI could provide a safety net for individuals who lose their jobs to automation and ensure that the economic benefits of technological progress are shared more widely.

2. Ensuring Fairness in the Workforce

Another key issue is ensuring that workers in **automated environments** are treated fairly. As robots and AI systems become more integrated into the workforce, there is a risk that human workers could be treated as secondary to machines, particularly in industries like customer service and logistics. The ethical question here is how to balance the use of automation with the fair treatment of human workers, ensuring that workers are not exploited or marginalized by automated systems.

For example, some automated systems, such as AI-driven customer service chatbots, have been criticized for providing a subpar customer experience compared to human agents. While automation can enhance efficiency, it is important that businesses do not sacrifice quality of service or worker satisfaction in the pursuit of cost reduction.

Accountability: Who Is Responsible for Automated Systems?

As machines become more autonomous, questions about accountability become increasingly complex. If a self-driving car causes an accident, for example, who is responsible? Is it the manufacturer of the vehicle, the software developer, the owner of the car, or the designer of the AI system? This question of **accountability** is a central ethical issue in the age of automation and robotics.

1. **Ethics of Autonomous Systems**

Autonomous vehicles and other self-driving technologies, such as drones and robots, raise important ethical concerns about responsibility in the event of accidents or malfunctions. In a traditional scenario, human drivers or operators are held responsible for their actions. But in the case of autonomous systems, the question of accountability becomes more complicated.

Some experts argue that manufacturers and developers of autonomous systems should be held accountable for ensuring that their technology is safe and reliable. Others suggest that as autonomous systems become more integrated into society, **new legal frameworks** will be necessary to determine liability in cases where accidents occur.

2. Ethical Decision-Making in AI Systems

Another ethical challenge involves the **decision-making processes** of autonomous systems. For example, in situations where a self-driving car must make a decision that could harm one person to save others, how should the system make that choice? This raises important questions about **moral responsibility** and **programming ethics** in AI systems. Some argue that these systems should be programmed with ethical guidelines to ensure that their decisions align with human values and societal norms.

For instance, should a self-driving car be programmed to prioritize the safety of its passengers, or should it be designed to minimize harm to others, even if it means endangering the passengers? These are complex ethical dilemmas that will require input from a wide range of stakeholders, including ethicists, engineers, policymakers, and the public.

Conclusion: Navigating the Ethics of Automation

As automation and robotics continue to advance, they bring with them both significant benefits and serious ethical challenges. The displacement of jobs, the fair distribution of automation's benefits, and the accountability of autonomous systems are key issues that must be addressed to ensure that automation works for the benefit of all.

To navigate these ethical challenges, it will be important for society to engage in open discussions about the impact of automation on work, fairness, and accountability. Policymakers, businesses, and workers must work together to create ethical frameworks that ensure the responsible use of technology and ensure that the benefits of automation are shared equitably across society. By doing so, we can ensure that automation enhances human life rather than replacing it, and that it contributes to a future that is both prosperous and just.

This chapter explores the ethical challenges posed by automation, including job displacement, fairness, and accountability. Let me know if you'd like to explore any aspect in more detail or add more examples!

CHAPTER 20

ROBOTICS IN THE HOME: AUTOMATION FOR EVERYDAY LIFE

Introduction: The Rise of Domestic Robots

In recent years, the integration of **automation and robotics** into our everyday lives has moved from the realm of science fiction to a tangible reality. While robots have traditionally been confined to industrial settings or research labs, they are now making their way into homes, transforming the way we live, work, and interact with technology. From **smart appliances** and **robotic assistants** to **home security robots** and **personalized health-monitoring systems**, automation is becoming an increasingly important part of daily life.

In this chapter, we will explore how automation and robotics are starting to infiltrate our homes, improving convenience, efficiency, and quality of life. We'll also examine the potential challenges and ethical considerations of welcoming robots into our personal spaces.

Smart Appliances: The Automation of Household Tasks

One of the most visible examples of automation in the home is the widespread use of **smart appliances**. These devices are connected to the internet and can be controlled remotely via smartphones, voice commands, or even through sensors that allow them to operate autonomously. Smart appliances are designed to make everyday household tasks more efficient and less time-consuming.

1. **Smart Kitchens**

The kitchen is one of the areas where automation is making the most significant impact. **Smart refrigerators**, **ovens**, and **dishwashers** are becoming increasingly common, and they offer a range of features that make cooking, cleaning, and food storage easier.

- **Smart Refrigerators**: Modern refrigerators now come equipped with features like touchscreens, cameras, and voice assistants. Some smart refrigerators can track the contents of your fridge, send alerts when items are running low, and even suggest recipes based on what you have available. Others can be controlled remotely, allowing you to

181

adjust the temperature or check the status of your groceries from anywhere.

- **Smart Ovens**: Smart ovens can preheat themselves, adjust cooking times and temperatures automatically, and allow you to control them remotely via apps or voice commands. Some models even feature built-in cameras that allow you to monitor your food as it cooks.

- **Smart Dishwashers**: Dishwashers now offer advanced features like auto-sensing technology that adjusts water usage and washing cycles based on the load. They can also be monitored remotely, ensuring that they are running efficiently.

By automating kitchen tasks, these smart appliances save time and energy, making it easier for individuals to manage their households and prepare meals with less effort.

2. Laundry and Cleaning Robots

Another area where automation is making a huge difference is in laundry and cleaning. **Robot vacuums**, such as the popular **Roomba**, have become a staple in many homes. These devices autonomously navigate through rooms, vacuuming floors, and avoiding obstacles. Some models are even equipped with advanced mapping technologies that allow them to clean efficiently and ensure that no area is missed.

Smart washing machines and dryers are also on the rise, offering features such as remote control, automatic cycle adjustments, and energy-saving settings. These machines can be operated from a smartphone app, allowing users to start, pause, or monitor the status of their laundry from anywhere, making laundry day a more streamlined process.

In addition to vacuums and washing machines, **robotic mops** and floor cleaners are becoming more advanced, capable of handling various floor types and cleaning specific areas with precision. These robots are becoming essential in maintaining a clean home without human intervention, offering a more convenient and efficient way to keep floors spotless.

Robotic Assistants: Personal Help in the Home

The development of **robotic assistants** has been a game-changer in home automation, offering more than just simple task management. These robots are designed to interact with humans, learn from their preferences, and carry out a wide range of tasks, from controlling smart devices to assisting with personal tasks.

1. Voice-Controlled Virtual Assistants

Devices like **Amazon Echo**, **Google Home**, and **Apple HomePod** have become integral parts of many households. These voice-controlled virtual assistants are capable of performing tasks such as controlling smart appliances, setting reminders, providing weather updates, and even ordering groceries. By using natural language processing (NLP), these assistants can understand and respond to a wide range of commands, making them useful tools for managing daily routines.

Some voice assistants are also integrated with AI-powered systems that allow them to learn user preferences and adapt over time. For instance, a smart assistant might learn to adjust your home's temperature based on your daily schedule or recommend music based on your listening history.

2. Humanoid Robots for Personal Assistance

In addition to voice-controlled devices, humanoid robots are becoming more advanced and capable of performing more complex tasks. For example, **Jibo**, a social robot, can interact with family members, play music, take pictures, and even tell jokes. Similarly, **Pepper**, a robot designed for human interaction, is used in some homes to provide companionship and assist with daily activities.

While these humanoid robots are still in the early stages of development, they represent a future where robots can serve as personal assistants in the home, offering help with everything from organizing tasks to providing emotional support.

Home Security Robots: Automation for Safety

Robotics and automation are also making homes safer through the development of **security robots** and **smart surveillance systems**. These technologies are designed to monitor homes, detect potential threats, and provide real-time alerts to homeowners or security teams.

1. Autonomous Security Robots

Some homes are now equipped with robots that patrol the property and perform surveillance tasks. These robots are equipped with cameras, motion sensors, and facial recognition software to detect unusual activity or intruders.

For example, **Knightscope** offers a line of autonomous security robots that can patrol properties and alert security teams to any threats.

These security robots can navigate around the home autonomously, using sensors to avoid obstacles and ensure complete coverage of the property. By automating surveillance, these robots provide an extra layer of security without requiring human intervention, improving the efficiency of home security systems.

2. Smart Doorbell Cameras and Security Systems

Another key area of home automation in security is the development of **smart doorbell cameras**, such as **Ring** and **Nest Hello**, which allow homeowners to monitor visitors at their front door from anywhere in the world. These devices include video cameras, motion detectors, and two-way audio, enabling users to communicate with visitors or delivery personnel remotely.

Integrated with home security systems, these devices help homeowners maintain a secure and connected environment.

The Ethical and Social Considerations of Home Automation

186

While the integration of automation and robotics into the home offers many benefits, it also raises important ethical and social considerations. Some of the primary concerns include:

1. **Privacy**: As robots and smart devices become more pervasive, concerns about data privacy and security have grown. Many smart home devices collect personal data, such as voice recordings, video footage, and usage patterns, which could potentially be accessed by unauthorized parties or exploited for commercial purposes. It is crucial for manufacturers to implement robust data protection measures and for users to understand how their data is being used.

2. **Job Displacement in Domestic Services**: The rise of household robots raises questions about the future of domestic work. While robots can improve efficiency, they may also lead to job displacement for domestic workers, such as housekeepers, cleaners, and nannies. As more households adopt automation, it will be important to address the social and economic impact of these changes on the labor market.

3. **Social Interaction**: While robots can provide assistance, companionship, and entertainment, there

are concerns about their impact on social relationships. In some cases, people may become overly reliant on robots for companionship or emotional support, potentially leading to social isolation or reduced human interaction.

Conclusion: The Future of Home Automation

Robotics and automation are transforming the way we live by making everyday tasks easier, safer, and more efficient. From smart appliances and robotic assistants to home security robots and automated cleaning systems, these technologies are enhancing the convenience of modern life and offering new levels of comfort and productivity.

As we embrace the benefits of home automation, it is important to consider the ethical, social, and economic implications of these technologies. With careful planning, thoughtful regulation, and a focus on inclusivity, automation can be integrated into our homes in ways that enhance quality of life while addressing the challenges posed by these advancements.

This chapter provides an overview of how automation and robotics are reshaping our homes and everyday lives. Let me know if you would like to explore specific areas in more detail or add more examples!

CHAPTER 21

ECONOMIC IMPACTS OF WIDESPREAD AUTOMATION

Introduction: The Global Economic Transformation Through Automation

The increasing adoption of automation across industries is set to have profound effects on global economies. While automation promises significant improvements in efficiency and productivity, its widespread implementation will also bring about fundamental changes in income distribution, economic growth, and employment patterns. From manufacturing to services, automation is reshaping how goods are produced, services are delivered, and economies operate.

In this chapter, we will explore how automation will reshape economies on a global scale. We'll look at its impact on productivity, income distribution, and economic growth, as well as the broader implications for labor markets, inequality, and global competitiveness.

Productivity Growth: The Driving Force of Automation

One of the most significant economic impacts of automation is its potential to **increase productivity**. By automating routine, repetitive, and manual tasks, businesses can achieve higher output with fewer resources. This efficiency boost allows companies to reduce costs, improve product quality, and increase production capacity, leading to higher overall economic output.

1. **Productivity Gains Across Sectors**

In sectors like manufacturing, agriculture, and logistics, automation allows for the continuous operation of machines, resulting in faster production cycles and a reduction in human error. For example, in **manufacturing**, automated robots can assemble products at a faster rate than human workers, enabling companies to scale up production without increasing labor costs. Similarly, in **agriculture**, robots that handle tasks like planting, harvesting, and irrigation are improving yields and reducing reliance on seasonal labor.

In **service sectors**, such as finance, healthcare, and retail, automation is driving productivity improvements by streamlining administrative tasks, improving customer

191

service, and optimizing inventory management. For instance, **AI-powered chatbots** in customer service can handle thousands of customer inquiries simultaneously, reducing wait times and freeing up human agents to focus on more complex issues.

The overall result of these productivity gains is higher output per worker, which can lead to **economic growth** and increased competitiveness, both for individual firms and national economies.

2. Impact on Economic Output and Competitiveness

At a macroeconomic level, productivity improvements driven by automation can boost **gross domestic product (GDP)** and improve a country's economic competitiveness on the global stage. Nations that adopt automation technologies early are likely to see a more rapid expansion of their industrial base, greater efficiency in resource use, and a rise in the overall standard of living.

For example, countries like **Germany**, which have been early adopters of industrial automation, have seen substantial increases in productivity in their manufacturing sectors, contributing to their competitive advantage in industries like automotive production. As automation becomes more widespread, it will be crucial for other countries to follow suit in order to maintain global competitiveness.

Income Distribution: Automation's Role in Inequality

While automation has the potential to increase overall productivity, it also brings with it significant **challenges to income distribution**. The economic benefits of automation are unlikely to be evenly shared across all sectors or population groups, and if not carefully managed, automation could exacerbate existing inequalities in wealth and income.

1. Job Displacement and Wage Polarization

One of the key challenges posed by automation is its potential to displace jobs, particularly those in low-wage and low-skill sectors. As robots and AI systems take over repetitive tasks, workers in fields like manufacturing, transportation, and customer service may find their jobs increasingly at risk. These workers often face significant barriers to entering more skilled professions, such as the need for advanced education or retraining.

In contrast, automation is likely to create high-paying jobs in sectors related to technology, robotics, and AI, where workers will need specialized skills. This could lead to a **wage polarization** effect, where workers with advanced technical skills enjoy higher wages, while those in lower-skilled jobs face stagnant wages or unemployment.

The shift toward high-skill, high-wage jobs and the displacement of low-skill workers may widen the **income gap** and contribute to rising economic inequality. Those who are able to adapt to the changing labor market may benefit from higher incomes, while others may struggle to maintain their standard of living.

2. Universal Basic Income and Redistribution Measures

To address the potential for increased inequality, some economists and policymakers have proposed solutions such as **universal basic income (UBI)** or **progressive taxation**. UBI involves providing every citizen with a fixed, unconditional cash payment, regardless of their employment status. The goal of UBI is to ensure a basic standard of living for all individuals, even as automation disrupts traditional employment.

Additionally, governments may need to explore **redistributive policies**, such as taxes on automation or wealth, to fund social safety nets and reskilling programs. By redistributing some of the economic gains from automation, it may be possible to mitigate the negative effects on income inequality and ensure that the benefits of automation are more widely shared.

Economic Growth: Automation's Potential to Drive Global Prosperity

While the distribution of automation's benefits remains a significant challenge, its potential to drive overall **economic growth** is immense. By improving productivity, reducing costs, and enhancing competitiveness, automation has the potential to accelerate economic growth both within individual countries and across the global economy.

1. **Raising Global GDP**

At a global level, widespread automation could lead to higher **global GDP** by enabling businesses to produce more goods and services at lower costs. As automation becomes more prevalent, countries with higher rates of adoption will see faster economic expansion. This increase in economic output will not only benefit businesses but could also result in lower prices for consumers, making goods and services more affordable and improving living standards.

For example, **China** has rapidly adopted automation in its manufacturing sector, allowing it to become a major player in global trade. As automation spreads to other countries, it will likely have similar effects on global production and consumption patterns, stimulating economic growth across the world.

2. The Role of Innovation and New Industries

Automation is also likely to foster **innovation**, leading to the creation of entirely new industries and business models. As robots and AI systems take over existing tasks, they will free up human workers to focus on more complex and creative endeavors. This could lead to the development of new technologies, services, and markets that were previously unimaginable.

For example, the rise of **autonomous vehicles** has the potential to create entirely new industries related to mobility, logistics, and transportation. Similarly, the automation of **healthcare** could lead to more personalized, efficient, and accessible care, creating new opportunities for both innovation and economic growth in the sector.

The Global Landscape: Automation's Impact on Developing Economies

While automation has the potential to drive growth in developed economies, its impact on **developing economies** is more complex. On the one hand, automation can help developing countries leapfrog traditional stages of industrialization, allowing them to quickly adopt advanced technologies without having to go through the same labor-intensive processes as more developed economies.

On the other hand, many developing countries rely on low-wage labor in sectors like agriculture, textiles, and manufacturing, which are most vulnerable to automation. If automation leads to job displacement in these sectors, it could exacerbate poverty and slow down economic progress in developing nations. International cooperation and investment in **education**, **infrastructure**, and **technology adoption** will be essential for ensuring that automation benefits developing economies and helps lift millions out of poverty.

Conclusion: Navigating the Future of Automation and Economic Change

The economic impacts of widespread automation are profound and multifaceted. While automation holds immense potential for driving productivity, reducing costs, and fostering innovation, it also presents significant challenges in terms of job displacement, income inequality, and economic disruption. To ensure that the benefits of automation are widely shared, it will be essential for governments, businesses, and workers to collaborate on solutions such as reskilling programs, social safety nets, and progressive economic policies.

By embracing the potential of automation while addressing its challenges, we can create a future where technology drives both economic growth and social well-being. The key to navigating this transformation will lie in finding ways to adapt and ensure that the economy remains inclusive, dynamic, and fair for all.

This chapter explores the economic impacts of automation, focusing on productivity, income distribution, and economic growth. Let me know if you'd like to explore specific aspects in more detail or add further examples!

CHAPTER 22

THE ROLE OF GOVERNMENT IN SHAPING THE FUTURE OF WORK

Introduction: Governments as Key Players in the Age of Automation

The rapid rise of automation and robotics is transforming industries and the nature of work itself. While these technological advancements offer immense potential for growth, efficiency, and innovation, they also present significant challenges. One of the most pressing issues is ensuring a **smooth transition** for workers and industries that are affected by automation. **Governments** play a crucial role in regulating automation, protecting workers, and ensuring that the economic benefits of automation are distributed fairly across society.

In this chapter, we will explore the various roles governments play in shaping the future of work, including **regulating automation**, **providing support for displaced workers**, and **ensuring that the benefits of automation are shared equitably**. We'll also examine the policies and strategies governments can adopt to guide the workforce through this period of technological transformation.

Regulating Automation: Setting the Framework for a Safe and Fair Transition

As automation technologies become more integrated into industries, governments must establish regulations that ensure these technologies are deployed safely and ethically. These regulations must address concerns related to **job displacement**, **safety standards**, and **data privacy**, while also promoting innovation and economic growth.

1. Regulation of Autonomous Systems

One of the most significant regulatory challenges associated with automation is the **integration of autonomous systems** (e.g., self-driving vehicles, drones, and robots) into public and private sectors. Governments need to develop frameworks to ensure that autonomous systems are safe for human interaction and comply with established rules and standards.

For example, self-driving cars pose unique challenges related to safety, liability, and traffic regulation. The **U.S. National Highway Traffic Safety Administration**

(NHTSA) has established guidelines for testing and deploying autonomous vehicles on public roads. Governments must also work with companies, experts, and citizens to establish laws governing the **responsibility** for accidents involving autonomous vehicles. These laws need to address questions of accountability, insurance, and ethical decision-making in the event of an accident.

Similarly, **AI-driven systems** and **robotic technologies** need to be monitored and regulated to ensure they do not infringe upon human rights, create bias, or compromise safety. Regulations on **data privacy** and the use of personal information in AI systems will be crucial in protecting citizens' rights and maintaining trust in these technologies.

2. Labor Laws and Worker Protection

As automation replaces jobs in various sectors, governments must also focus on updating **labor laws** to protect workers' rights in an automated world. Existing labor laws were designed for a workforce that predominantly involved human labor, but these laws need to evolve to address the changing nature of work.

Governments will need to update laws related to **worker classification**, ensuring that gig and freelance workers— whose jobs are often mediated by automated platforms—are treated fairly. This includes ensuring that workers have access to benefits such as healthcare, retirement savings, and paid leave, even if they are not full-time employees.

Moreover, **safety regulations** in workplaces where robots and humans coexist will be essential. Governments will need to enforce standards for **human-robot interaction** to ensure the safe use of robots in manufacturing, construction, and other industries. For example, robots that work alongside human employees in factories must be designed with safety features to avoid accidents.

Supporting Workers: Providing Transition Programs and Safety Nets

The displacement of workers due to automation presents a significant challenge for governments. While automation has the potential to create new jobs, it also leads to the loss of jobs in traditional industries. Governments must develop **social safety nets** and **transition programs** that help workers adapt to the changing labor market.

1. Reskilling and Retraining Programs

One of the most important roles governments can play is providing **reskilling and retraining opportunities** for workers whose jobs are threatened by automation. By offering access to **education and training** in high-demand fields such as **AI**, **data science**, **cybersecurity**, and **renewable energy**, governments can ensure that workers can transition to new roles without facing long periods of unemployment.

Public-private partnerships will be key to developing effective reskilling programs. Governments can collaborate with businesses, educational institutions, and technology providers to create training programs that are tailored to the needs of the workforce. For example, **Amazon Web Services (AWS)** offers a cloud computing training program in partnership with governments, providing workers with skills needed for jobs in the tech sector.

Additionally, governments can provide **financial support** to workers while they are retraining, through programs like **unemployment benefits** or **subsidized education**, to ensure that individuals have the resources they need to transition smoothly into new careers.

2. Universal Basic Income (UBI)

As automation potentially leads to the displacement of large numbers of workers, some have proposed **Universal Basic Income (UBI)** as a solution. UBI is a policy in which every citizen receives a fixed, unconditional payment from the government, regardless of their employment status. The goal of UBI is to provide a basic standard of living for all individuals, ensuring that even if people lose their jobs due to automation, they still have financial support to meet their basic needs.

Pilot programs for UBI have been conducted in countries such as Finland, Canada, and the United States, with promising results in reducing poverty and improving mental health. While UBI is not a one-size-fits-all solution, it could be an important tool for governments to use in ensuring that workers are supported during times of economic transition.

Ensuring Fairness: Addressing the Distribution of Automation's Benefits

As automation increases productivity and economic output, there is a risk that the benefits will not be distributed fairly across society. Governments must take steps to ensure that the **economic gains** from automation are shared equitably, preventing further concentration of wealth and power among a small number of corporations and individuals.

1. Progressive Taxation and Redistribution

Governments can consider **progressive taxation** policies that ensure that companies that benefit most from automation contribute to the social safety net. This includes taxing the profits of corporations that benefit from increased productivity due to automation and redistributing these funds to support displaced workers, invest in public goods, and fund reskilling programs.

Taxing automation itself—specifically the use of robots and AI systems that replace human workers—has been proposed as a way to fund programs like UBI and reskilling initiatives. By taxing automation, governments can ensure that businesses benefiting from technological progress contribute to the welfare of workers affected by these changes.

2. Promoting Inclusive Growth

Governments must also focus on promoting **inclusive growth**, ensuring that the benefits of automation reach all segments of society. This includes providing access to technology, education, and job opportunities in rural and underserved communities. In addition to investing in **reskilling programs**, governments can create incentives for businesses to invest in automation technologies that create jobs in emerging industries, such as **green energy** or **clean technology**.

Supporting entrepreneurship in the age of automation is another important aspect of promoting inclusive growth. Governments can encourage the creation of small businesses and startups in sectors that are less vulnerable to automation, such as creative industries, healthcare, and the arts.

Conclusion: Governments Shaping the Future of Work

Governments play a crucial role in shaping the future of work in an era of rapid automation. By implementing smart regulations, supporting workers through reskilling and safety nets, and ensuring that the benefits of automation are equitably distributed, governments can help guide societies through the complexities of technological transformation.

The future of work will require a collaborative approach, where governments, businesses, workers, and other stakeholders work together to address the challenges and seize the opportunities of automation. With thoughtful policies and a focus on fairness and inclusion, automation can be a force for good, driving productivity and economic growth while ensuring that all citizens benefit from the changes that are reshaping the world of work.

This chapter highlights the important role of government in regulating automation, protecting workers, and ensuring a smooth transition into a more automated world. Let me know if you'd like to explore further areas or examples!

CHAPTER 23

BUILDING A SUSTAINABLE FUTURE IN AN AUTOMATED WORLD

Introduction: Automation as a Driver of Sustainability

As the world grapples with challenges such as climate change, resource depletion, and environmental degradation, the role of **automation** in achieving sustainability is becoming increasingly significant. While automation has often been associated with increased efficiency and productivity, it also has the potential to be a powerful tool for promoting **environmental sustainability**. By optimizing resource use, reducing waste, and creating more sustainable production processes, automation can play a crucial role in building a **sustainable future**.

In this chapter, we will explore how automation can contribute to sustainability, focusing on areas such as **waste reduction**, **energy efficiency**, and **resource management**. We will also examine the potential of automation to address some of the most pressing environmental issues facing the planet, from carbon emissions to the responsible use of natural resources.

Automation and Waste Reduction: Minimizing Environmental Impact

1. Smart Manufacturing and Circular Economy

One of the primary ways automation can contribute to sustainability is by promoting **efficient production** processes that reduce waste. In traditional manufacturing, the production of goods often results in a significant amount of **material waste** and **energy consumption**. However, with the help of **automated systems**, manufacturers can produce goods more efficiently, using fewer resources and generating less waste.

For example, **smart manufacturing** systems that use **artificial intelligence (AI)** and **machine learning** can predict production needs with high accuracy, reducing the overproduction of goods and the associated waste. These systems can also **optimize material use**, ensuring that the raw materials are used in the most efficient way possible, which can lead to less scrap material and reduced energy consumption.

210

The concept of the **circular economy**—where products are designed for reuse, recycling, and regeneration—can also be enhanced by automation. Automated systems can help in the sorting, disassembly, and processing of materials for recycling. For instance, **robots** and **AI-powered systems** can be deployed in recycling plants to separate different types of waste, such as plastics, metals, and paper, with greater accuracy and efficiency than manual methods.

2. Automated Waste Management Systems

In urban environments, waste management is a critical area where automation can drive sustainability. **Automated waste collection** and sorting systems can help reduce the environmental impact of waste disposal. Drones, robots, and smart bins are being used to collect waste and recyclables more efficiently, reducing the need for labor-intensive manual collection and minimizing the carbon footprint of waste management operations.

For example, in cities like **Seoul** and **Singapore**, **automated waste collection systems** have been implemented, where robots can collect waste from residential areas or industrial complexes and transport it to designated facilities. These systems are equipped with sensors and GPS to optimize collection routes and ensure that waste is properly sorted and processed.

Energy Efficiency: Automation in Renewable Energy and Resource Conservation

1. Smart Grids and Energy Management

Energy use is one of the largest contributors to environmental degradation, particularly in the form of **carbon emissions** from fossil fuels. However, automation is playing a key role in improving **energy efficiency** and promoting the adoption of **renewable energy** sources. **Smart grids**, for example, are automated systems that use sensors, data analytics, and AI to optimize the generation, distribution, and consumption of energy in real-time.

Smart grids can help integrate renewable energy sources, such as **solar** and **wind power**, into the energy mix by adjusting power generation and distribution to match fluctuating supply and demand. Automation also allows for **energy storage** systems to be better managed, ensuring that excess energy produced by renewable sources can be stored for later use, reducing the reliance on non-renewable sources.

2. Automated Energy-Efficient Buildings

Automation also plays a crucial role in creating **energy-efficient buildings**. **Building automation systems (BAS)** are designed to control a building's heating, ventilation, air conditioning (HVAC) systems, lighting, and other energy-consuming systems. These systems can be controlled remotely and programmed to adjust based on occupancy or environmental conditions, optimizing energy usage and reducing waste.

For example, **smart thermostats** can automatically adjust indoor temperatures based on the number of people in a room or the time of day, reducing the amount of energy used for heating and cooling. Similarly, automated lighting systems can turn off lights in rooms that are not in use or adjust brightness levels based on natural light, reducing electricity consumption.

Resource Management: Automation in Agriculture and Water Conservation

1. Precision Agriculture: Optimizing Resource Use

Agriculture is another key area where automation is driving sustainability. **Precision agriculture** uses automated

213

systems to monitor and manage crops with a high degree of accuracy, minimizing the use of water, fertilizers, and pesticides. **Drones**, **sensors**, and **AI-powered systems** can collect data on soil conditions, weather patterns, and crop health, helping farmers make better decisions and reduce the environmental impact of farming.

For example, **autonomous tractors** can optimize planting patterns and adjust planting depth and spacing based on soil conditions, leading to better yields and reduced resource consumption. **Automated irrigation systems** can also monitor soil moisture levels and apply water precisely when and where it is needed, minimizing water waste and improving crop health.

2. Water Management: Automating Conservation Efforts

Water scarcity is one of the most pressing challenges in many parts of the world, and automation can play a key role in **water conservation**. **Smart irrigation systems** use sensors to measure soil moisture and weather conditions, ensuring that water is only applied when necessary. These systems help reduce water waste in agriculture, landscaping, and even urban areas by optimizing water distribution.

Automated **water treatment plants** also offer potential for improved water conservation and efficiency. These plants use automated systems to monitor water quality, detect contaminants, and adjust filtration processes in real time, ensuring that water resources are used efficiently and safely.

Automation in Sustainable Supply Chains

1. **Supply Chain Transparency and Optimization**

Another significant area where automation contributes to sustainability is in **supply chain management**. By using automation, companies can improve the efficiency of their supply chains and reduce their carbon footprint. **AI-powered systems** can predict demand more accurately, reducing the need for overproduction and unnecessary transportation. These systems also enable companies to track the environmental impact of their supply chains, allowing them to make more informed decisions about sourcing materials, transportation, and waste reduction.

For example, companies like **Walmart** and **Amazon** are using AI and robotics to optimize their supply chains, improving product distribution while reducing waste and energy consumption. By integrating **sustainability metrics** into their supply chain management systems, these companies can ensure that their operations align with environmental goals.

The Future of Sustainable Automation

The future of automation holds significant potential for contributing to a more sustainable world. As technologies continue to evolve, there will be new opportunities to improve resource management, reduce waste, and promote the adoption of renewable energy sources. Innovations in **robotics**, **AI**, and **IoT** will further enhance our ability to automate sustainability efforts across sectors, from agriculture to energy.

However, as we increasingly rely on automation for sustainability, it is important that we also address the **ethical** and **economic** implications of these technologies. Governments, businesses, and individuals must work together to ensure that the environmental benefits of automation are realized without exacerbating inequalities or causing unintended harm.

Conclusion: Automation as a Catalyst for Sustainability

Automation holds the key to addressing many of the world's most pressing environmental challenges. By improving resource management, reducing waste, and optimizing energy usage, automation has the potential to drive a **sustainable future** in which technology and nature coexist harmoniously. Through innovation, collaboration, and careful planning, automation can be a powerful tool in creating a greener, more sustainable world for future generations.

This chapter explores how automation and robotics contribute to sustainability, from waste reduction to resource management. Let me know if you'd like to dive deeper into any specific example or area!

CHAPTER 24

THE FUTURE OF REMOTE WORK IN AN AUTOMATED WORLD

Introduction: The Rise of Remote Work and Automation

Remote work has experienced a significant transformation in recent years, accelerated by technological advancements and the global shift caused by the COVID-19 pandemic. The ability to work from anywhere, thanks to cloud computing, video conferencing, and collaboration tools, has become the norm for many employees worldwide. However, as **automation**, **robotics**, and **artificial intelligence (AI)** continue to evolve, the landscape of remote work is undergoing yet another profound change.

Automation is not just about machines replacing human labor; it's about enhancing productivity, optimizing workflows, and creating opportunities for employees to focus on high-value tasks. As automation and AI technologies integrate into remote work environments, they offer both challenges and opportunities. This chapter explores how these technologies are reshaping the future of remote work, enabling more efficient and flexible work arrangements, while also raising new questions about work-life balance, job roles, and worker well-being.

Automation and AI: Enhancing Productivity in Remote Work

1. AI-Powered Tools for Remote Work

One of the primary ways automation and AI are reshaping remote work is through the development of advanced **AI-powered tools** that enhance productivity and streamline workflows. From **AI-based scheduling assistants** to **intelligent collaboration platforms**, these tools are transforming how remote teams communicate, manage tasks, and collaborate across time zones.

For instance, AI-driven virtual assistants, like **Google Assistant**, **Cortana**, and **Siri**, can help remote workers schedule meetings, manage their calendars, and send reminders, reducing the time spent on administrative tasks. Similarly, AI tools like **Grammarly** assist with writing, while project management tools like **Asana** and **Trello** leverage automation to streamline task assignments, progress tracking, and deadline management.

Intelligent Collaboration Tools powered by AI can help teams manage workflows more efficiently by automatically sorting emails, suggesting responses, and even identifying priorities based on the context of the conversation. These tools make remote work smoother by automating routine tasks, allowing workers to focus on higher-level problem-solving and strategic thinking.

2. **Automated Document Management and Data Analysis**

Automation is also enhancing the management and analysis of data for remote teams. With **cloud-based document management systems**, automation allows documents to be automatically stored, organized, and categorized without human intervention. Systems like **Dropbox** or **Google Drive** not only store data but can also employ AI algorithms to help workers search for and retrieve documents more effectively.

Automated data analysis tools are further changing the remote work landscape by enabling employees to gain insights from large datasets without needing to manually sift through the information. Tools like **Power BI**, **Tableau**, and **Google Analytics** use AI to generate reports, identify trends, and present actionable insights in a user-friendly way. These capabilities empower remote workers to make data-driven decisions without the need for specialized data analysis skills, increasing efficiency and productivity.

3. **Chatbots and Virtual Customer Service Assistants**

Remote work in customer service, sales, and support is increasingly relying on **chatbots** and **virtual assistants** powered by AI. These systems can handle routine customer inquiries, process orders, and even provide product recommendations, allowing human agents to focus on more complex issues.

For example, **Zendesk** and **Intercom** offer AI-powered customer service platforms that help automate responses to frequently asked questions, while **chatbots** engage customers in real-time, providing assistance 24/7. By using automation in this way, businesses can improve customer satisfaction and support their remote teams by reducing the volume of repetitive work.

Robotics: Transforming Remote Work in Industrial and Specialized Settings

1. Remote-Controlled Robotics in Manufacturing and Warehousing

Although much of the automation that enables remote work is focused on office-based tasks, **robotics** is also reshaping industries where remote workers can control and operate machines from a distance. In sectors like manufacturing, logistics, and warehousing, robots can perform physical tasks such as assembly, packaging, and material handling with minimal human involvement.

Teleoperated robots allow workers to control machines remotely, increasing safety and efficiency in environments where human presence could be dangerous, such as in hazardous manufacturing settings or warehouses. For example, companies like **Vecna Robotics** and **Locus Robotics** are using **autonomous mobile robots (AMRs)** in warehouses that can be controlled remotely, enabling warehouse staff to oversee operations from home or another safe location.

This trend is expected to continue as robots become more capable of performing complex tasks autonomously. Workers in industries like **construction** and **healthcare** are also benefiting from remote-controlled robotic systems that allow them to perform jobs from a safe distance while still maintaining control and oversight.

2. Robots in Healthcare: Remote Surgery and Telemedicine

The rise of robotics and AI is also transforming **healthcare**, with remote work playing an increasingly important role in providing healthcare services. **Robotic surgery systems** such as **Intuitive Surgical's Da Vinci** allow surgeons to perform complex procedures remotely using robotic arms controlled by the surgeon's movements. Surgeons can operate from a different location, improving access to healthcare in remote or underserved areas.

Telemedicine, which allows doctors to consult with patients remotely, is also benefiting from automation. AI-powered systems can analyze patient data, monitor vital signs, and make recommendations, allowing healthcare professionals to provide care remotely. This reduces the need for in-person visits, making healthcare more accessible while enabling medical professionals to work remotely.

Work-Life Balance: The Impact of Remote Work and Automation on Employee Well-Being

While automation and remote work offer significant benefits in terms of productivity and flexibility, they also raise concerns about the **work-life balance** of employees. The ability to work from home, combined with AI tools and automation, means that workers can be constantly connected, making it harder to separate personal time from professional responsibilities.

1. The Potential for Overwork and Burnout

With AI and automation handling many routine tasks, there is a risk that remote workers could find themselves expected to take on more work or be available around the clock. The boundary between work and personal life can become blurred, leading to **overwork** and **burnout**.

To address this, companies must be proactive in creating boundaries for remote workers. This could include setting clear expectations for work hours, ensuring regular breaks, and fostering a culture that encourages employees to unplug when they are not working. Automation tools that manage scheduling, set reminders for rest, and track productivity can also help employees manage their workloads and avoid burnout.

2. Fostering Connection and Collaboration in Remote Teams

One of the challenges of remote work is maintaining strong **team collaboration** and **employee engagement**. Automation and AI can help bridge the gap by facilitating communication and ensuring that remote teams stay connected. Tools like **Slack**, **Microsoft Teams**, and **Zoom** use AI to optimize meeting scheduling, transcribe discussions, and even generate summaries, helping to ensure that all team members are on the same page, regardless of location.

While these tools are essential for remote collaboration, they must be used thoughtfully to avoid creating a sense of isolation among employees. Companies should encourage regular check-ins, virtual team-building activities, and social interactions to ensure that remote workers feel connected and supported.

The Future of Remote Work in an Automated World

The future of remote work will be one where **automation**, **AI**, and **robotics** are seamlessly integrated into the work environment. As automation handles routine tasks and optimizes workflows, employees will have more time to focus on creative, strategic, and high-value activities, leading to greater job satisfaction and innovation.

At the same time, it is crucial for governments and companies to address the potential challenges of automation in remote work, including job displacement, overwork, and the digital divide. By investing in education, reskilling, and supportive policies, we can ensure that the benefits of automation are accessible to all workers, regardless of their role or industry.

Conclusion: Embracing the Opportunities of Remote Work and Automation

The combination of remote work and automation is shaping the future of the workplace. Automation is making remote work more efficient, flexible, and productive, enabling workers to collaborate and innovate from anywhere in the world. As technology continues to evolve, the potential for remote work to become a permanent feature of the global workforce grows, offering workers greater freedom and companies greater efficiency.

However, as we embrace these opportunities, it is essential to ensure that automation is used ethically, with a focus on employee well-being, job security, and equitable access to technological tools. By carefully managing these shifts, we can build a future where remote work and automation create a more productive, sustainable, and inclusive global workforce.

This chapter explores how automation and robotics are reshaping remote work, providing new opportunities and challenges for both employers and employees. Let me know if you'd like to dive deeper into any specific area or example!

CHAPTER 25

THE PSYCHOLOGICAL IMPACT OF AUTOMATION ON WORKERS

Introduction: The Human Side of Automation

The rise of automation and robotics has undoubtedly transformed industries, increased productivity, and improved efficiency. However, the psychological impact of automation on workers is a less frequently discussed but critically important aspect of this technological shift. As robots and AI systems increasingly take over routine, manual, and even complex tasks, workers are faced with feelings of **job insecurity**, **stress**, and **identity loss**. The disruption caused by automation may lead to changes in mental health, job satisfaction, and overall well-being, both for those whose jobs are replaced and for those working alongside automated systems.

In this chapter, we will explore how automation and robotics can affect the **psychological health** and **job satisfaction** of workers. We will examine the emotional and cognitive responses to automation, how workers may cope with these

228

changes, and the potential long-term effects of automation on the workforce's mental health.

Job Insecurity and Fear of Displacement

1. Fear of Job Loss

One of the most significant psychological impacts of automation is **job insecurity**. As robots and AI systems become more capable, workers may fear that their jobs will be replaced. This fear can lead to anxiety, stress, and a sense of **loss of control** over one's professional future. For example, in industries like **manufacturing, transportation**, and **retail**, where automation is already making significant inroads, workers may worry that their roles will become obsolete.

The prospect of being replaced by a machine can be particularly daunting for individuals whose jobs are highly specialized or routine-based, and for whom retraining or transitioning to another role may seem difficult. This sense of **uncertainty** can create chronic stress, erode job satisfaction, and diminish workers' overall well-being. Even employees in industries where automation is more gradual may experience anxiety about future job security as they witness the growing trend of technological advancement.

2. Impact on Motivation and Engagement

The fear of displacement doesn't just affect the emotional well-being of workers—it can also have a tangible impact on their **motivation** and **engagement**. If employees believe their jobs are at risk due to automation, they may become **disengaged** from their work, feeling that their efforts no longer matter in the long term. This can lead to a **reduced sense of purpose** in their roles and a lack of enthusiasm for their daily tasks.

In addition, workers who feel their contributions are undervalued in an automated environment may be less likely to take initiative, collaborate, or strive for improvement. This disengagement can negatively affect workplace **culture** and **productivity**, creating a cycle of low morale that can extend beyond the affected workers to others within the organization.

Identity and Purpose: The Role of Work in Personal Fulfillment

1. Loss of Identity and Purpose

For many people, work is not just a source of income; it is also a significant part of their identity and sense of purpose. Automation can threaten this sense of identity, particularly for workers whose roles are being replaced by machines. If a worker's job is central to their self-esteem and social identity, losing that job to automation can lead to a **crisis of purpose** and a **loss of self-worth**.

In industries such as **healthcare, education**, and **public service**, where human empathy, creativity, and expertise are central to the work, automation may not replace jobs entirely but could still alter the way workers engage with their roles. This change may leave workers questioning their relevance or contribution in an increasingly automated environment. The psychological toll of **identity loss** can lead to **depression, anxiety**, and a sense of **disconnect** from the broader societal contribution of work.

2. Changing Roles and Evolving Work Expectations

As automation evolves, it can also change the nature of existing roles, making them more collaborative with robots and AI systems. For example, workers may transition from performing manual tasks to overseeing or managing automated systems. While this can create new challenges, it also opens the door for workers to **develop new skills** and evolve professionally.

However, the transition to these new roles can be emotionally challenging. Workers may feel **ambivalent** or **overwhelmed** as they adapt to the shifting demands of their positions. There may be an increased sense of **pressure** to quickly acquire new skills and knowledge in order to stay competitive. This adjustment period can be psychologically taxing, particularly for older workers or those with limited access to reskilling opportunities.

Stress and Anxiety: Coping with Technological Change

1. Technological Overload and Anxiety

The rise of automation can contribute to **technological overload**, a phenomenon in which workers are overwhelmed by the constant introduction of new tools and technologies. For many workers, the **integration of automation** into daily work tasks may feel like a relentless barrage of new systems to learn, coupled with the pressure to keep up with technological advancements.

This anxiety can be particularly acute in **remote work environments**, where employees often feel they are constantly connected and expected to be available at all times. AI-driven productivity tools, communication platforms, and project management systems can add pressure to maintain high levels of productivity, further contributing to stress and burnout.

Additionally, workers may experience **imposter syndrome**, feeling that they are incapable of mastering new tools or adapting to new roles, leading to a lack of confidence in their abilities. This can decrease overall **job satisfaction** and contribute to **mental health challenges** such as **burnout** and **depression**.

2. **Workplace Relationships and Collaboration with Machines**

As robots and AI systems become more integrated into the workplace, employees may face challenges in adapting to new **collaborative dynamics**. In settings where humans work side by side with machines, there is potential for **social isolation**, as workers may find it difficult to relate to or communicate with robots. This disconnection can also affect collaboration within human teams, as workers may feel less engaged or valued when their tasks are increasingly automated.

For example, if a human worker is tasked with overseeing a robot that performs the majority of a task, the worker may feel a lack of autonomy or contribution. While automation can enhance efficiency, it can also reduce opportunities for workers to engage in meaningful and creative aspects of their roles, further eroding job satisfaction.

The Role of Organizations in Supporting Mental Health in an Automated World

1. Creating Supportive Work Environments

Given the psychological challenges that automation can pose, it is crucial for **employers** to create supportive work environments that help workers adapt to technological changes. This includes offering **mental health resources**, such as counseling, stress management workshops, and **employee assistance programs** (EAPs), to help workers cope with anxiety, job insecurity, and identity loss.

Companies can also support their workers by offering **reskilling and upskilling** opportunities that provide workers with the tools they need to succeed in an automated workplace. By offering accessible training programs and clear career progression paths, businesses can mitigate the stress associated with automation and help workers feel more confident in their roles.

2. Fostering a Positive Culture of Automation

To improve job satisfaction and reduce anxiety, employers can foster a **positive culture** around automation by emphasizing its role as a tool that enhances human capabilities, rather than replaces them. By promoting a collaborative environment where automation is viewed as a partner to human workers, employers can reduce feelings of displacement and increase workers' sense of control.

Engaging workers in discussions about how automation will be integrated into their work and offering opportunities for feedback can help them feel more included in the decision-making process. Transparency and open communication are essential in ensuring that workers feel supported and valued during times of change.

Conclusion: Navigating the Psychological Impact of Automation

As automation continues to shape the future of work, it is essential to understand and address its psychological impact on workers. While automation offers significant benefits in terms of efficiency and productivity, it also poses challenges related to job insecurity, identity, stress, and mental health. Employers, policymakers, and workers must work together to navigate these challenges, ensuring that automation leads to a future of work that is both productive and psychologically healthy.

By prioritizing worker well-being, fostering supportive environments, and providing the tools for successful adaptation, we can ensure that the rise of automation leads to a more inclusive, satisfying, and mentally healthy workforce.

This chapter explores the psychological impact of automation on workers, covering the emotional responses, challenges, and coping mechanisms associated with automation in the workplace. Let me know if you'd like to expand on any section or explore additional examples!

CHAPTER 26

REAL-WORLD SUCCESS STORIES OF AUTOMATION

Introduction: Automation as a Catalyst for Innovation and Growth

As automation and robotics continue to evolve, many companies and industries are realizing the immense potential these technologies offer. From increased productivity and reduced costs to improved safety and enhanced customer satisfaction, automation is transforming the way businesses operate. While the adoption of automation has its challenges, numerous real-world examples demonstrate how companies have successfully integrated robotics, AI, and automated systems into their operations, leading to positive outcomes.

In this chapter, we will highlight several companies and industries that have embraced automation, showcasing the tangible benefits they've achieved, from improved operational efficiency to enhanced employee satisfaction. These success stories provide valuable lessons and offer a glimpse into the future of automation across various sectors.

1. Amazon: Revolutionizing E-Commerce and Logistics with Robotics

One of the most well-known examples of successful automation integration is **Amazon**, which has embraced robotics and automation at nearly every stage of its operations. The company has incorporated robots in its **warehouses, distribution centers**, and **delivery networks**, streamlining processes and improving efficiency in ways that would have been unimaginable just a few years ago.

1. Robotic Warehouses

Amazon's **fulfillment centers** have become a model for how robotics can revolutionize logistics. Amazon employs **Kiva robots** (now known as **Amazon Robotics**) that autonomously navigate the warehouse floor, transporting goods and sorting inventory. These robots reduce the time it takes for workers to locate and retrieve items, significantly improving the speed of order fulfillment.

Amazon's use of robots allows the company to handle millions of orders each day while ensuring that workers remain safe and efficient. The robots handle tasks such as sorting, lifting, and moving heavy items, which reduces the physical strain on human workers and enhances overall productivity.

2. Automated Delivery and Drones

Amazon is also exploring the future of automated delivery. The company's **Prime Air** drone delivery system aims to deliver packages to customers within 30 minutes using autonomous drones. Although still in the testing phase, this innovation could dramatically reduce delivery times, making Amazon even more competitive in the e-commerce space.

Positive Outcomes:

- Reduced delivery times and operational costs.
- Increased efficiency and productivity in warehouses.
- Improved worker safety by delegating physically demanding tasks to robots.
- Enhanced customer satisfaction with faster shipping.

2. Tesla: Pioneering Automation in Electric Vehicle Manufacturing

Tesla, a leader in electric vehicles (EVs), is another prime example of a company that has successfully integrated automation into its operations. Tesla's factories, known for their innovative production methods, use a combination of robotics, AI, and automated systems to manufacture high-quality electric cars at scale.

1. Automated Assembly Lines

Tesla's **Gigafactories** utilize highly automated assembly lines where robots perform tasks such as welding, painting, and installing components with incredible precision. The automation of these processes has allowed Tesla to achieve **rapid production rates** while maintaining high levels of quality control.

For instance, the company uses **robotic arms** to handle delicate parts of the assembly process, including fitting batteries into the vehicle chassis. These robots can operate 24/7, significantly increasing production capacity while reducing the potential for human error.

2. AI-Driven Quality Control

Tesla also employs AI-driven systems for quality control. Using cameras and sensors, the company's AI system scans the cars on the assembly line for defects, ensuring that only the highest quality vehicles reach customers. This automation of quality checks reduces the need for manual inspections and improves consistency across the production process.

Positive Outcomes:

- Increased production capacity and faster manufacturing cycles.
- Reduced error rates and improved quality control.
- Enhanced scalability in the production of electric vehicles.
- Continuous innovation in manufacturing and vehicle development.

3. Siemens: Automating Industrial Manufacturing for Efficiency and Precision

Siemens, a global leader in automation technology, has successfully integrated robotics and automation into its own manufacturing processes, setting a benchmark for the industrial sector. The company uses its own **advanced automation systems** in manufacturing facilities, applying these technologies to improve production efficiency, precision, and safety.

1. **Digital Twin Technology in Manufacturing**

Siemens utilizes **Digital Twin** technology, which creates virtual replicas of physical assets, processes, and systems. This allows Siemens to simulate entire production systems, analyze data, and optimize operations before implementing changes in the physical world. By using **digital simulations**, the company can test different configurations, predict outcomes, and make more informed decisions, leading to better resource utilization and reduced waste.

2. Collaborative Robots in Manufacturing

Siemens also employs **collaborative robots (cobots)** that work alongside human operators to increase efficiency and safety on the production floor. These cobots perform tasks like assembly, sorting, and material handling, while human workers focus on more complex and value-added activities. The robots are equipped with sensors and advanced AI algorithms that enable them to adapt to their environment and interact safely with humans.

Positive Outcomes:

- Improved manufacturing efficiency and reduced downtime.
- Enhanced precision and quality control.

- Increased safety for workers in potentially hazardous environments.
- Reduced resource waste and optimized use of materials.

4. Starbucks: Enhancing Customer Experience with AI and Robotics

In the food service industry, **Starbucks** has embraced automation to improve both the efficiency of its operations and the customer experience. The company has integrated AI-driven technologies and robotics into various aspects of its business, from ordering to delivery.

1. Robotic Baristas

In some of its stores, Starbucks has introduced **robotic baristas** that can prepare coffee and other beverages with high precision. These robots are designed to complement human workers by handling the repetitive task of brewing coffee, allowing baristas to focus on more complex orders or engage with customers.

2. AI for Personalized Customer Service

Starbucks has also implemented AI-powered systems for **personalized recommendations** and **order predictions**. Through its mobile app, customers can place orders in advance, and the AI system suggests drinks based on previous preferences, enhancing customer satisfaction and streamlining the ordering process.

Positive Outcomes:

- Faster order processing and reduced wait times for customers.
- Enhanced customer satisfaction with personalized recommendations.
- More efficient store operations, allowing employees to focus on customer engagement.

5. Walmart: Integrating Automation in Retail Operations

As one of the world's largest retailers, **Walmart** has been at the forefront of integrating automation into its operations, particularly in its supply chain and in-store processes.

1. **Automated Warehouses and Inventory Management**

Walmart has implemented **automated systems** in its distribution centers, where robots handle tasks such as sorting, packaging, and stocking inventory. This has significantly improved the speed and accuracy of inventory management, enabling faster replenishment of products on store shelves.

2. Self-Checkout Systems

In its stores, Walmart has deployed **self-checkout kiosks** that use automation to scan and process items, reducing long checkout lines and improving efficiency. The system can also detect and prevent fraud through advanced sensors and AI technology, providing a seamless customer experience.

Positive Outcomes:

- Faster inventory management and product restocking.
- Enhanced customer experience with self-checkout options.
- Reduced operational costs and improved store efficiency.

Conclusion: The Path to a More Automated Future

These real-world success stories demonstrate how automation and robotics are driving positive change across industries. From improved **efficiency** and **productivity** to enhanced **customer satisfaction** and **employee safety**, automation offers substantial benefits to businesses that embrace these technologies. While challenges remain, such as workforce displacement and the need for reskilling, these success stories illustrate that automation is not just about replacing jobs—it's about creating a future where technology enhances human capabilities, improves operations, and fosters innovation.

The companies highlighted in this chapter show that the integration of automation can be a win-win for both businesses and employees, as long as it is approached thoughtfully and strategically. As automation continues to evolve, more industries will adopt these technologies, and the positive outcomes of this shift will become even more apparent.

This chapter showcases how automation and robotics have successfully been integrated into various industries, providing tangible benefits. Let me know if you'd like more details on specific examples or other success stories!

CHAPTER 27

LOOKING AHEAD: THE NEXT FRONTIER OF WORK IN A ROBOTIC WORLD

Introduction: The Future of Work in a Robotic World

As automation and robotics continue to advance, the future of work is evolving at an unprecedented pace. From AI-driven technologies and autonomous robots to fully automated systems, the next frontier of work will be characterized by a deeper integration of machines into human tasks, reshaping industries, and the nature of work itself. The possibilities seem limitless, with new innovations emerging every day, but with these advancements come new challenges, opportunities, and questions about the future of human labor.

In this chapter, we will speculate on the next steps for automation and robotics in the workplace, discussing emerging trends, technologies, and the long-term implications for the workforce. As we explore this future, it is important to consider not only the technological advancements but also the social, economic, and ethical dimensions that will shape the way we work.

1. Fully Autonomous Workplaces: The Rise of the Machine-Run Office

One of the most significant developments on the horizon is the creation of **fully autonomous workplaces**, where machines handle almost every aspect of business operations. In these environments, robots and AI systems will manage tasks ranging from administrative duties and customer service to manufacturing and supply chain management, with little to no human intervention.

1. AI and Robotics in Decision-Making

In the future, AI systems will play a much larger role in **decision-making processes**. As AI becomes more sophisticated, machines will be able to analyze vast amounts of data, identify trends, and make informed decisions in real-time. In some cases, these systems may even be able to make strategic business decisions, from adjusting pricing models to forecasting market trends.

For example, AI-powered algorithms could be used to optimize supply chains by analyzing data from inventory

The Future of Work

systems, weather patterns, and customer behavior. Robots could autonomously adjust production schedules or reorder materials as needed, without the need for human oversight. This type of automation will allow businesses to operate with incredible efficiency, but it will also require significant changes in management structures and decision-making roles.

2. The Autonomous Office: Robots as Colleagues

In fully automated workplaces, robots will not just be tools—they will be colleagues. **Collaborative robots (cobots)** will work side by side with humans, taking on more routine tasks while allowing employees to focus on higher-level, creative, and strategic activities. These robots will have the ability to adapt to their environment, learning from their interactions with humans and other machines, and collaborating in real-time.

In an office setting, robots might handle tasks like scheduling meetings, organizing emails, and managing documents. At the same time, AI-powered virtual assistants will manage tasks such as drafting reports or analyzing data, freeing employees from administrative work and allowing them to engage in more meaningful, human-centric tasks.

2. The Evolving Role of Humans in an Automated Workforce

As robots take on more tasks, the role of humans in the workforce will shift. **Human creativity, empathy,** and **problem-solving** will become even more important in a world where machines handle routine and repetitive tasks. While automation will displace some jobs, it will also create new ones that require advanced skills, emotional intelligence, and complex decision-making abilities.

1. Human-Machine Collaboration

The future of work will be one of **collaboration** between humans and machines, with humans providing the **creativity, strategic thinking,** and **emotional intelligence** that machines currently cannot replicate, and machines providing the **efficiency, precision,** and **speed** that humans cannot achieve alone.

In the **creative industries,** for instance, humans will continue to drive innovation, design, and ideation, while machines will assist with data analysis, content creation, and even personalized recommendations. In sectors like **healthcare,** doctors and nurses will rely on AI to help with diagnoses, treatment plans, and robotic surgeries, while focusing on providing personalized care and managing patient relationships.

2. New Job Roles and Skills Development

As automation takes over many routine tasks, new job roles will emerge that require humans to manage, maintain, and interact with automated systems. For example, **AI trainers** will be needed to teach AI systems how to understand and interpret human behavior, while **robot maintenance engineers** will be in high demand to ensure that robots continue to function properly.

Additionally, the growth of automation will necessitate **continuous learning** and **reskilling** programs for workers, as they transition into new roles. Workers will need to adapt to a world where technological proficiency, problem-solving, and critical thinking are essential. **Lifelong learning** will become the norm, with workers regularly upgrading their skills to keep up with advancements in automation and AI.

3. The Impact of AI and Robotics on Workplace Culture

The integration of AI and robotics will significantly impact **workplace culture**. As automation changes the way employees interact with their work, organizations will need to reconsider how they approach employee engagement, collaboration, and leadership.

1. Remote and Hybrid Work Environments

Automation will likely enable even more widespread adoption of **remote** and **hybrid work** models. Robots and AI systems will help facilitate seamless communication and collaboration, making it easier for employees to work from anywhere in the world. **Virtual assistants** will manage daily schedules, video conferences, and task delegation, creating a more flexible and autonomous work environment.

However, this shift may also create new challenges related to **worker isolation**, **mental health**, and **work-life balance**. While automation can provide more flexibility, employees may struggle with the feeling of being constantly connected and available, leading to burnout and stress. Companies will need to find ways to foster a positive workplace culture and support employees' emotional and mental well-being.

2. Employee Autonomy and Job Satisfaction

As automation takes over many mundane tasks, workers will be freed to engage in more **meaningful** and **creative** work. This increased autonomy could lead to higher levels of **job satisfaction** and **engagement**, as employees are empowered to focus on tasks that require **human intuition, innovation,** and **critical thinking**.

However, it will be crucial for organizations to ensure that employees are not displaced by automation but are instead integrated into higher-level roles that leverage their unique human skills. A focus on **employee empowerment, leadership development,** and **skills-based roles** will be essential to maintaining job satisfaction in an increasingly automated world.

4. Ethical and Societal Considerations in the Future of Work

As automation becomes more pervasive, ethical considerations will be crucial in shaping the future of work. Issues such as **job displacement, privacy concerns,** and the **equitable distribution of benefits** from automation will need to be addressed to ensure a fair and just transition to a more automated society.

1. **Universal Basic Income (UBI) and Social Safety Nets**

With the potential for large-scale job displacement, some have proposed solutions such as **Universal Basic Income (UBI)** to ensure that individuals have access to basic resources, regardless of their employment status. UBI could provide a safety net for workers whose jobs are replaced by automation, allowing them to pursue new opportunities or engage in creative or entrepreneurial endeavors.

2. **Ethical AI and Automation Policies**

Governments, businesses, and regulatory bodies will need to establish ethical frameworks to guide the development and deployment of AI and robotics. These policies will need to address issues related to **bias in AI systems**, **data privacy**, and **responsibility** in decision-making. Ensuring that AI and robots are developed in ways that are **ethical, transparent**, and **accountable** will be crucial to maintaining trust in these technologies.

Conclusion: Embracing the Future of Work with Automation

The future of work in a robotic world will be shaped by collaboration between humans and machines. Automation will revolutionize industries, enhance productivity, and open up new possibilities for work. However, it will also present challenges, including job displacement, ethical dilemmas, and changes in workplace culture.

By embracing the potential of automation, fostering human-machine collaboration, and ensuring that the benefits of automation are equitably distributed, we can create a future of work that is more efficient, fulfilling, and sustainable. The key to navigating the next frontier of work will be a balanced approach—one that leverages the strengths of both humans and machines to create a thriving, adaptable workforce.

www.ingramcontent.com/pod-product-compliance
Lightning Source LLC
LaVergne TN
LVHW051443050326
832903LV00030BD/3215